LITTLE BOOK OF THE

GRAND NATIONAL

Written by Julian Seaman
Foreword by Richard Pitman

G2 rights ltd

www.G2rights.co.uk

Little Book of the Grand National
First edition published in the UK in 2015
© G2 Rights Limited 2015

Print Edition ISBN: 978 178 2811 923

G2 Rights Ltd, 7-8 Whiffens Farm, Clement street, Hextable, Kent BR8 7PQ

Contents

Facts in History

Foreword

Julian Seaman's book on the Grand National has slotted in superbly with my extensive Aintree library collected over five decades of personal involvement which started when lining up in 1967 for a race which has since become folklore and known simply as "Foinavon's year".

Two second places were the closest taste of world wide recognition in horsey circles that I managed as a jockey but the subsequent years as part of the BBC television team gave me real insight to the ever changing fortunes of this unique contest.

Julian has hit exactly the right note in this book retaining the dreams, the fairy tales, the swift, unexpected departure of millions of punters' dreams and the amazing leaps of faith that come from man (and some women) and their horses. Yet he has sniffed out numerous facts and situations that I knew nothing of despite it being the only subject I could have asked for on Mastermind!

I applaud his diligence and know the army of followers of this test of man/horse over the marathon trip and tricky questions the fences pose, will find so much more than was contained in any single previous Grand National recollection.

How apt that the sponsors of The National from 2014 are Crabbie's who produce a ginger beer - as ginger is known to settle your stomach, while the race itself has the opposite effect!

Julian has captured the flavour perfectly.

Richard Pitman

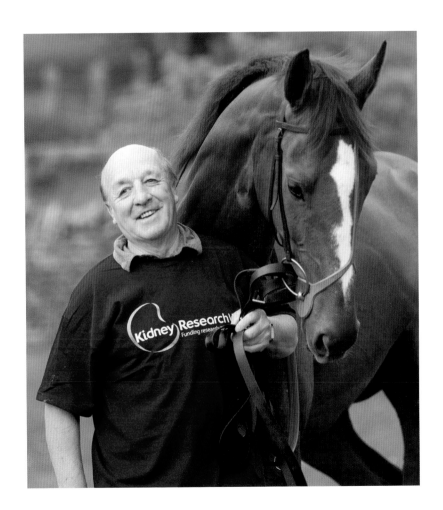

Introduction

The Grand National is the most famous horse race in the world, watched on television by an estimated 600 million people. Since its first official running in 1839 there have been some amazing tales of good and bad luck; jockeys brave to the point of lunacy; heroes and villains; weird coincidences; void races; bomb scares; fairy tales and nightmares; top pros and plucky amateurs; pioneering lady riders and trainers.

Every year seems to throw up a story. In Little Book of the Grand National I have distilled some of the one-off quirks in the history of the great race in bullet-point form, and expanded on some of the more famous stories that have arisen over the years. Two weighty tomes I have consulted in depth are A Race Apart, the History of the Grand National, by Reg Green (Hodder and Stoughton), and A-Z of the Grand National, John Cottrell and Marcus Armytage (Highdown).

I am also indebted to Jane Clarke (archivist for Aintree) for providing support, help and expertise. Richard Duplock also has given great encouragement to this enterprise.

A Little Book by nature is not a full coverage of the event, for which the two mentioned publications are excellent, and in this modern age all previous results, records and data can be found online.

This book is a primer full of golden nuggets to show why the Grand National is such a magical horse race.

The Grand National early years

William Lynn, the landlord of the Waterloo Hotel, Ranelagh Street, Liverpool, leased land at Aintree from William Molyneux, the second Earl of Sefton, with the idea of running some flat races. He set out a course and on 7 February 1829 the earl laid the foundation stone for the grandstand. Aintree was so named after a Viking settlement where the invaders had cleared the forest and left just one tree: Ain Tree.

By 1835 there was an all-hurdling card at the Aintree October meeting and winning two races on the same horse, Vivian, on the same day was the most celebrated cross country rider of the time, Captain Martin Becher. Steeplechasing was still in its early years. There had been a Steeplechase at St. Albans for five years. William Lynn put one on at Aintree in February 1836. This was also won by Becher, riding The Duke. To some purists this is thought of as the very first Grand National. However for the next two years what was now titled The Grand Liverpool Steeplechase was not run at Aintree, but at nearby Maghull.

In 1836 the entrepreneurial Lynn inaugurated a popular hare coursing event to entice more clients to his hostelry. This became the Blue Riband of the sport, known as the Waterloo Cup, and was run at

Above:
Great Liverpool
Steeplechase 1839

Great Altcar until 2005 when the sport was banned.

In 1839 Lynn was somewhat muscled out of his involvement with horse racing at Liverpool when the grandees, Lords Sefton, Derby, Bentinck, Stanley and Grosvenor put together a syndicate and took the event back to Aintree.

The 1839 race is generally accepted as the first running of the Grand National. This race was over a distance of more than four miles across open country. Most of the jumps were two-foot banks topped with gorse with ditches either in front or behind. There were one or two posts and rails and a 4'8"

9

Above:
Captain Becher
in the brook

wall. There were also two brooks; the first was dammed to produce an eight-foot spread behind a 3'6" post and rails.

During the race, coming to the first brook, Capt. Becher was disputing the lead when his horse Conrad put on the brakes, sending his rider over his head and into the freezing water. The fence was duly christened Becher's Brook. He later remarked of his soaking, 'Water should never be taken without brandy.' After remounting he fell at the next brook.

That, however, found its name

Above:
The Stone Wall

the following year when the hard-pulling Valentine ground to a halt, clambered over the fence intact and went on to finish third.

The first winner of the Grand National was Lottery ridden by Jem Mason.

Becher had paraded his unit of the Duke of Buckingham's Yeomanry at the coronation of king George IV. He ended his career as an inspector of sacks for Great Northern Railway and retired to Maida Vale in London.

In 1841 the wall was replaced by a ten-foot wide water jump.

The course initially included quite a lot of plough and was only railed in and fully turfed by 1885.

The race was now well established, but William Lynn, without whose foresight the whole spectacle would never had come to fruition, died a pauper in 1870, shunned by the aristocrats who tasked themselves to turning what had been seen as something of a disreputable sport into a more gentlemanly affair.

Right:
*Lottery and
Jem Mason*

Far Right:
Tom Olliver

Facts in History

One of the top early jockeys was Tom Olliver, known as 'Black Tom' from his swarthy Spanish gypsy background. He won in 1842 and 1843 on Gay Lad and Vanguard and again in 1853 on Peter Simple.

The race first became a handicap in 1843. The first handicapper was Edward Topham.

In 1843 the Wall was reintroduced. It was thought horses crashing through stone would be a crowd pleaser. It wasn't. Owners and riders, too, were less than impressed.

Lottery, the first winner, ended his days pulling a cart in Neasden, North London.

In 1843 the race was renamed the Liverpool and National Steeplechase. In 1844 the wall was replaced again with a post and rails.

In 1845 after winning, Cure-All, who had walked all the way from (Grimsby) Lincolnshire to Liverpool was walked back home from Aintree by his dedicated groom Kitty Crisp to a hero's welcome.

Although referred to as The Grand National from its start, it was first officially called The Grand National Handicap Steeplechase in 1847.

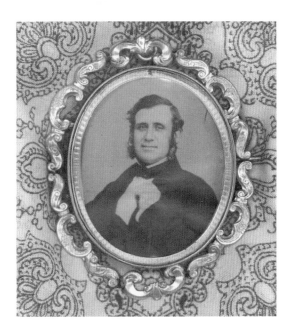

Right:
*Count Charles
Kinsky and
Zoedone*

International runners

For the purpose of this section the Irish don't count as foreign as at the time they were Britsih anyway.

They were represented at the first race in 1839 and were as instrumental as the English in the establishment of the sport of steeplechasing. They had a first winner of many in the race in 1847 with Matthew.

The first proper foreign challenge in 1856 was from France, albeit with an English trainer, Harry Lamplugh, who sent over two, Franc Picard and Jean du Quesne, neither of whom completed. Six years later Lamplugh won as a jockey on French owned Huntsman, but he had been English bred and previously owned. English owned and trained but French bred Alcibiade in 1865 and Reugny in 1874 also won but for this exercise let us consider foreign owned, trained or ridden challengers, some of whom finalised their preparations with English trainers, but were essentially challenges from abroad. Under this rule Austrian Count Charles Kinsky qualifies even though he was on an English bred and trained Zoedone to win in 1883. They were fifth a year later.

English and Irish contestants held sway for the next 65 years, then in 1904 Moifaa, New Zealand owned and bred, came home with a very generous weight of 10st7lbs ahead of the king's Ambush II, who was giving him almost two stone. The weight issue was surprising in some ways. The horse had won under heavy weights in his home country, but his prep runs in England were unimpressive, so he was generously handicapped. Most other foreign challengers, with no

Right:
Mrs. Randolph Scott

English form, were automatically given top weight. The reputed best jumper in Europe, L'Africaine, was lumbered with 13st 2lbs in 1866, and the following year France's Astroblade got top weight and again in 1868, along with the first Hungarian entry, Buszke.

French owned La Veine came third in the colours of Baron Finot in 1875. In 1889 German bred Et Cetera, owned by Hungarian Count Nicholas Esterhazy, attracted the market but fell under G Morris. In 1899 the popular French sportsman Count de Geloes rode his own mare Pistache, who fell.

There were no serious foreign challengers for several decades but there was considerable interest when, at the height of the Cold War, there were two entries from Soviet Russia in 1961, Reljef and Grifel. Both 100-1 outsiders, Reljef unseated B. Ponomarenko and V. Prakhof pulled up Grifel.

Many of the brave challengers came to grief. Japan's 1966 entry Fujino-O refused for Jeff King. In 1986 Russian bred and Czech ridden Essex pulled up. There has been sensible interest in Czech participation as they run arguably a more testing race in the Velka Pardubicka, and stars of that contest have every right to tackle Aintree. They have yet to shine however. These were Valencio, 1987; Fraze, 1991 and Quirinus in 1994.

The French got the hang of racing their horses in England prior to the race to achieve a sensible handicap, and in 1909 the Mnsr. James Hennessy owned Lutteur III came in under Georges Parfrement carrying 10st 11lbs.

In the 1920s and 1930s there was considerable American ambition to win the race. Sergeant Murphy triumphed in 1923 for Mr. Stephen Sanford under Capt. Geoffrey 'Tuppy' Bennet. Sanford had two

runners in 1926, Mount Etna and Bright's Boy. The spoils went, however, to another American entry, Jack Horner, who had come seventh the previous year under his sporting American owner, Morgan de Witt Blair, now owned by well known US polo player Charles Schwartz and ridden by Tasmanian born jockey, William Watkinson, who had come second in 1922 on Drifter. In 1933 Kellsboro Jack ran in the colours of Mrs. Florence Ambrose Clark, wife of US sewing machine millionaire F. Ambrose Clark (who had "bought" the horse from her husband for one pound in the hope of changing his previous bad luck). He also had a runner in Chadd's Ford. The wife's horse won.

These American victories were English trained, but in 1938, under the glamorous ownership of Hollywood's Mrs. Randolph Scott, US-bred and trained Battleship, all of 15.2 hh, came in under Bruce Hobbs.

The preparation was meticulous and the horse had raced considerably in England prior to the tilt at the National.

Later it was the turn of two sporting American amateurs. In 1965 Jay Trump lined up. He had been bred in Pennsylvania by Mr. Jay Sessenich and was a flop on the flat. He was bought for Mrs. Mary Stephenson by top American amateur Crompton 'Tommy' Smith, with the ambition of lifting their premier timber race, the Maryland

Hunt Cup, which they duly won twice. Next stop Aintree. Doing a proper job they took themselves off to be prepared by Fred Winter. They had three wins under their belt before lining up at Aintree. Hotly pursued by Freddie in the run-in, Smith reverted to the whip nearly with disastrous consequences. Jay Trump took exception to the interference and started swishing his tail and swerving about. The rider put his whip down and rode hands and heels to win by just three quarters of a length.

In 1979 Baltimore investment banker Charlie Fenwick put the diminutive Ben Nevis with Tim Forster, and was well up in the betting for Aintree. They were brought down in a nine horse pile up at The Chair. Fenwick remounted, but pulled up soon after.

It was a different story the following year. Ben Nevis, like Jay Trump, had won the Maryland Hunt Cup on two occasions. Fenwick was riding

Facts in History

In 1859 attempts were made to reduce some of the obstacles the night before. Lord Sefton put a stop to the skulduggery.

In 1862 young Irish rider James Wynne, son of 1847 winning rider Denny, heard that his sister had died on the morning of the race. His mount's owner tried to persuade him not to ride in the race but to return home. Young Wynne was determined however. He fell at the fence before the water and was subsequently rolled on by another faller. He died that night.

1863 saw the distance of the course extended to a full four and a half miles, though apart from Becher's and Valentine's most of the fences were still quite small.

There was a ditch and bank to be tackled in 1864.

Alcibiade won the race on his debut over fences in 1865. He was ridden by Captain Coventry of the Grenadier Guards on his first attempt.

The Grand Military meeting was held at Aintree in 1867 following the Wednesday National, giving three full days of racing.

Above:
Amateur Charlie
Fenwick wins with
Ben Nevis

for his father in law, Redmond C. Stewart Jnr. At the second Becher's, Delmoss was upside Ben Nevis and well clear of the rest of the field. Delmoss fell leaving Fenwick twelve lengths ahead, and although John Francome was making some progress on Rough and Tumble, there was no danger. Ben Nevis eventually won by 20 lengths.

Number of entries

Since 1984 the maximum number of runners in the Grand National has been kept at 40, however this restriction has varied over the years. Of course, not all horses entered get a run, and many forfeit the first stage of the entry fee once the weights have been announced by the handicapper.

In recent years over a hundred have put down their deposit and a high point was reached in 2005 with 152 entries for the 40 places. The entries for the early April race close in January, with the weights being announced in February.

In the first 90 years of the race the most runners was 32, in 1850. There were only ten in 1883, 11 in 1841, 12 in 1878 and 1882 and 13 in 1840. With some 1920s races only getting a handful of finishers, and no-hoper, 100-1 outsider Tipperary Tim

winning in 1928, many owners and trainers decided it was worth having a go, so in 1929 a vast field of 66 horses lined up at the start. Oddly enough, another 100-1 outsider, Gregalach, came in. Numbers thereafter began to stabilise at between 30 and 40.

With racing abandoned during the Second World War after the 1940 race, there was an upsurge of interest after hostilities and in

Below:
A record
66 starters
in 1929

the spring of 1947 a big freeze put early racing on hold. Owners and trainers wanted a run for their horses and eventually 57 turned up to post. That turned out to be a bit of a one-off and numbers again became more manageable.

In 1960, because of safety concerns, qualifications were tightened up and only 26 came forward. The following year however the sloping "aprons" were introduced on the take-off side of the obstacles, making the course substantially more forgiving, encouraging larger, faster (if higher quality) fields. In 2003 trainer Martin Pipe entered no fewer than 19 horses at the first stage. In 2008 one owner, J.P. McManus, entered 11.

Facts in History

The course was properly measured for the first time in 1868 and it came just 30 yards short of four-and-a-half miles.

Large boulders marked the route out into the country in 1868 and, before the race had even started, the favourite, Chimney Sweep, broke his leg connecting with one and had to be put down.

In 1870 George Stevens rode his fifth winner of the race on The Colonel, on whom he had also succeeded the previous year. George Ede (Mr. Edwards) was set to retire soon after the 1870 race, as he had just become engaged, but he was persuaded to ride in a one-circuit race the day after the National. He was advised not to take the ride on Chippenham by his friend Arthur Yates, who warned: 'Don't ride the brute, George, he will kill you.' He still took the ride, had a bad fall at the fence before the water, and died. Ede was a founder of Hampshire Cricket Club, for whom he was a prolific batsman.

Devon Loch

The Queen Mother's horse was one of the most spectacular losers of the race.

He was ahead after the last fence and had no serious challengers, when inexplicably he spreadeagled within sight of the winning post under the jockey Dick Francis, later to become a racing thriller writer in conjunction with his wife. Many theories have been expounded: that he jumped a shadow, that he was startled by the cheers of the crowd. But writer Graham Lord has a more prosaic theory.

He reckons that the horse's girth was tightened too much before the start and Devon Loch had a build up of intestinal gasses that exploded in a massive fart so that 'He was lifted clean off the ground like a half-ton rocket.'

Facts in History

The Lamb, leased by Lord Poulett, had won the race with George 'Mr. Edwards' Ede in the saddle in 1868. After Ede's tragic death in 1870, the owner had a dream that his small grey would win again with the other famous alias rider Tommy 'Mr. Thomas' Pickernell on board in 1871. Poulett booked Pickernell for the ride in a letter, swearing him to secrecy about the dream. They duly won.

After his 1871 win The Lamb had much of his tail hacked off by souvenir hunters on his way to the winning enclosure.

The winning horse in 1870, The Colonel, retired to Germany and became a charger for Kaiser Wilhelm I.

The 1872 winner, Casse Tete, was owned by a Mr.Brayley, who had started his theatrical career as a Punch and Judy man.

John Maunsell Richardson, an Old Harrovian, won on Disturbance in 1873 and Reugny the following year. He went on to become a prominent racing writer, as did Old Etonian winner Marcus Armytage over a century later.

Tommy 'Mr. Thomas' Pickernell liked a little tipple to steady the nerves before the race, but in 1875, at the age of 41, he slightly over did it. He had to ask fellow jockeys which way to point at the start. Once away however nothing could stop him and Pathfinder coming home in front.

Aristo riders: *The Marquess of Waterford came fourth in 1840 on The Sea*

Aristo riders: *Viscount Megrund who rode under his Eton nickname of Mr.Rolly. He fell from Zero in 1876. It was thought he had broken his neck, but it 'clicked' back into place.*

Aristo riders: *Count Metternich, tenth on Brigand in 1879.*

Aristo riders: *Lord Manners, who won the race in 1882 on Seaman.*

Family connections

Only one father and son have won the Grand National as riders, Tommy Carberry on L'Escargot in 1975 and Paul Carberry with Bobbyjo in 1999.

Tom Rimell trained Forbra in 1932 and his son Fred triumphed three times as a trainer with ESB in 1956, Gay Trip in 1970 and Rag Trade in 1976.

Seven fathers have trained winners ridden by their sons:

Rubstic in 1979 on one of only three rides in the race. Both father and son Pitman. Richard-Steel Bridge (1969), Crisp (1973) and Mark-Garrison Savannah, (1991) have finished second.

Three generations of Scudamores – Michael, Peter and Tom – have ridden in the race, and it could have been four if the War

Left:
Peter Scudamore

Left:
Tom Scudamore

John and Garrett Moore, the Liberator (1879); John and Arthur Nightingall, Ilex (1890); Tom and Ted Leader, Sprig (1927); Noel and Frank Furlong, Reynoldstown (1935); Reg and Bruce Hobbs, Battleship (1938); Tommy and Paul Carberry, Bobbyjo (1999); and Ted and Ruby Walsh, Papillon (2000).

Tommy Barnes came second on his only ride, Wyndburgh, in 1962 and his son Maurice won on

had not prevented great grandfather Geoffrey from taking part.

Ginger McCain trained Red Rum in 1973, 1974 and 1977 and Amberleigh House in 2004, while his son Donald handled Ballabriggs in 2011.

Martin Pipe had Miinnehoma (for comic Freddie Starr) in 1994 and son David saw in Comply or Die in 2008.

John Alder came ninth as an amateur in 1965 on his own Tant Pis and his daughter Valerie got as far as the Canal Turn in 1984 on Bush Guide, while Nina Carberry completed with Forest Gunner in 2006 after her father had won with L'Escargot (1975) and her brother with Bobbyjo (1999).

Facts in History

Aristo riders: *Count Charles Kinsky won on Zoedone the year after Lord Manners, prompting pro Jimmy Adams to remark, ' Last year it was A blooming Lord won the National; this year it's a f***ing count and next year it will be an old woman most likely.' Overhearing this the count countered, 'Yes Jimmy, and I hope this old woman will be yourself.'*

In 1877 the amateur rider Fred Hobson had a bizarre riding style where he would grab the front of the saddle when going over a jump. His excuse was that doing this and leaning well back would take the strain off the horse's shoulders. His detractors put it down to fright. Advised by many of his friends not to ride his own horse, Austerlitz, in the 1877 race, the pair won nonetheless.

In 1878 a fire started under the Royal Box just before the parade, but was quickly put out.

In 1879 half of the 18 riders were amateur, including four Beasley brothers from Ireland.

Irish trainer Henry Linde built a replica Aintree course on his gallops at The Curragh. He trained up Empress before selling her to a Mr.Ducrot just before the 1880 running. She duly came in with Tommy Beasley up.

By 1883 entries for the race were substantially down and an inquiry revealed that a gradual easing of the jumps had led critics to suggest that the race was no longer a great test of jumping but just a long distance gallop. Crowd control was also a problem, with spectators ambling on to the course. To an extent these were rectified for the race that year.

What had always been seen as a slightly disreputable sport had an image boost in 1884 when the Prince of Wales entered The Scot. His horse Leonidas had won the Military Hunt Steeplechase at Tweseldown in 1840, but this was its first entry for the top chase in the world. It fell.

Facts in History

The 1884 winner Voluptuary had previously run a rather poor Derby in 1881. After winning the National he was bought by a well known actor, Leonard Boyne, who jumped him nightly over a water jump on the stage of the Drury Lane Theatre in a production of The Prodigal Daughter. He returned to the National in 1889 and 1890 to fall and in 1891 to be knocked over.

In the early days of the race there was a practice hurdle on the way to the start.

A mare called Frigate was second in 1884 under H. Beasley and again the following year. She fell in '86, pulled up in '87, second again under W.Beasley in '88 and finally won it in 1889 under T. Beasley. Back again,the pair fell in 1890.

The 1887 winner Gamecock came out the next day to win the Champion Steeplechase under 12st 12 lbs.

In 1888 the final bend on the course cut the corner. It only cut the distance by about 25 yards, but the final two obstacles, which had been hurdles, were now proper fences.

The winning rider in 1888, George Mawson had a lucky escape. Nearly being unseated two before Becher's, he was scooped back into the saddle by fellow jockey Arthur Nightingall. Nightingall won the race himself on Ilex in 1890, Why Not in 1894 and Grudon in 1901.

Harry Beasley, who rode in the race with his three brothers in 1879, lived until 1939. He rode in his last race, the Baldoyle Corinthian Plate, in 1935 at the age of 85.

The owner of the 1896 race winner, The Soarer, Mr. Hall-Walker gave a large proportion of his betting win to Liverpool Art Gallery, which became the Walker Gallery. He also donated his stud in Ireland to the nation, which became the Irish National Stud.

Manifesto, who first won in 1897, became something of a National hero winning again in 1899 when giving a stone to his rivals. He contested a record eight Grand Nationals, finishing in seven of them and, in1902, came third ridden by Lester Piggott's grandfather, Ernie.

The Prince of Wales led his own Ambush II into the winner's enclosure in 1900. The Prince had a good racing year with his Diamond Jubilee taking the triple crown of the 2,000 Guineas, Derby and St. Leger.

Ambrose Gorham, owner of the 1902 winner, Shannon Lass, left the whole village of Telscombe to the Brighton Corporation with the following stipulation: 'I direct the Corporation shall prefer a man who is a sportsman and not a total abstainer from alcohol and tobacco.

'1903 saw the first entry from a reigning British monarch with King Edward VII's Ambush II. He fell.

Both Drumree and Drumcree contested the 1903 race. Coming to the last Drumcree was just ahead of Drumree, though the latter was going better. Then Drumree had a fit of the staggers and fell on the flat, a precursor to the Devon Loch disaster that was to happen 53 years later. Drumcree won.

In 1904 a New Zealand horse Moifaa was entered. He had won a three-and-a-half milechase at home under 13 st. He had three moderate runs before Aintree, and being a strong puller pretty well jumped through the fifth where several of the runners fell. Moifaa won by

eight lengths. He was subsequently bought by Edward VII to run the following year. (The King had previously described the horse as having the 'head and shoulders of an overstuffed camel'). Moifaa fell in 1905.

The first past the post in 1905 was the riderless Ascetic's Silver. He won it for real the next year with Mr. Hastings on board.

In 1907 jockey Alfred Newey broke a stirrup leather early in the race riding Eremon. Over Becher's they were back in contention, but were being baulked by a loose horse, Rathvale, and Newey had to use his whip to shoo him away at the Canal Turn. He continued to do this for much of the remainder of the race. By Valentine's on the second circuit the stirrupless Newey was 20 lengths clear and eventually won by six.

An American-bred horse called Rubio only fetched fifteen guineas as a yearling at Newmarket. He broke down after some races in 1903. To get him sound again an unlikely regime was employed. He went to the Pomfret Arms at Towcester and was used to pull the hotel bus from the station. He returned to training in 1906 and won the National in 1908.

Facts in History

The 1909 race was won by French jockey Georges Parfrement, who looked at many maps of the course before the challenge, and lengthened his stirrups before the big race. He triumphed on Lutteur III.

It was bad luck for trainer Frank Bibby in 1910 when the least fancied of his runners, Wickham, took both his stable companions Glenside and Caubeen out of the race - however matters were to right themselves the following year when Glenside won.

It was once said that: 'The object of the Aintree fence builder's art was one day to eliminate the entire Grand National field.' In 1911 the only horse not to part company with his rider was the one-eyed Glenside who came in with Mr. J.R. (Jack) Anthony up. Three others finished with remounted jockeys. For once the old adage that, 'There are fools, damn fools and men who remount in steeplechases.' was proved wrong.

A miners' strike in 1912 played havoc with the steam-train timetables and there was a worry that the National would not be able to run. It did, but infront of the smallest ever crowds. Lester Piggott's grandfather, Ernie, scored the first of his three Grand National wins (one of these a "War substitute" at Gatwick) on Jerry M.

In 1913 jockey Percy Woodland scored on chance ride Covertcoat ten years after winning on another chance ride, Drumcree. Only three finished, with Carsey remounted by Mr. Tyrwhitt-Drake.

Though the Great War was underway the race was still run at Aintree in 1915. Ally Sloper was led in by the first female owner, Lady Nelson.

During the First World War a substitute race was held at what is now Gatwick Airport in 1916, 1917 and 1918.

Dorothy Paget

Below:
Dorothy Paget
leads in Golden
Miller 1934

Dorothy Paget was one of racing's great characters in the inter-war years. Born in 1905, she was the only daughter of Lord Queensborough. Having gone to smart girl's boarding school

Heathfield, in Ascot, her later eccentricities showed early flowering. Having trained as a singer, her first gig was in front of 500 prisoners at Wormwood Scrubs Prison. She then went to be 'finished' in France and set up a colony of exiled Russian aristocrats. At 21 she inherited a fortune from her mother's side of the family, and decided to sponsor a team

of racing Bentleys at great expense. This was not an entirely successful venture, since her team never won anything substantial, so she decided to swap her enthusiasm from horsepower to horse racing, one of her father's passions. He had won the 1922 2,000 Guineas with St Louis.

She spent a great deal of money on horses that failed to make a return, notably Tuppence, bought for 6,000 guineas, who failed to impress in the 1933 Derby and was subsequently sold for £300, and, worse than that, the 15,000-guinea yearling purchase, Colonel Payne, who then was sold for just 250 guineas ten years later. She did however have some remarkably lucky breaks. At a London card game in 1931 trainer Basil Briscoe persuaded Miss Paget to part with £12,000 for a job lot of two horses. Insurance promptly won the following Champion Hurdle and became the first horse to win the race back to back in 1933. The other

horse in the package was none other than the great Golden Miller. His Cheltenham debut was also to be in 1932, in the Gold Cup. Both trainer and jockey Ted Leader thought the going too firm to run the promising 13-2 five-year-old, but Miss Paget, no doubt in emboldened betting-mode after her Champion Hurdle success, had her money on, and insisted he ran. This was to be the first of his amazing five wins of the race in a row.

Dorothy, who always liked to surround herself with a bevy of attentive female secretaries, had a great sporting rivalry with her American cousin Jock Whitney, who had seen his colours come second at the Grand National in 1929 with Easter Hero, and third the following year with Sir Lindsay. The National was Paget's abiding ambition, which she duly realised in 1934 when 'The Miller' achieved the Cheltenham-Aintree double. He won the

National in the then-fastest time. Dorothy had a massive celebratory party at Liverpool's Adelphi Hotel that night.

Despite running in five Nationals, Golden Miller never repeated the success. Paget had runners in 13 Nationals including the 8-1 favourite in 1939, Kilstar who came third under American jockey, George Archibald. The following year, when there was still some racing despite the War, Paget had the Gold Cup and Champion Hurdle winners.

She also had success on the flat

when Straight Deal won her the Derby in 1943. After the War, when racing resumed at Aintree, Dorothy had several other runners including the 1952 runner-up, Legal Joy, and another second the following year with her 1952 Gold Cup winner Mont Tremblant.

Friends of Dorothy and her many trainers and bookmakers could be exasperated by her strange lifestyle and hours. She tended to sleep during the day, having breakfast at eight-thirty at night and dinner at seven in the morning, and insisted on having long discussions with her trainers at all hours. She also had an amazing relationship with her bookies, who let her put large wagers on races that had already been run. They trusted her to not know the results, and indeed she often incurred substantial losses! She was a keen trencherwoman, rising up to 20 st, and died in her sleep in 1960 aged 54.

Facts in History

In 1919 the outsider All White was due to carry only 9st 10lbs. His usual lightweight jockey was injured so a jockey called Tommy Williams ate hardly anything in the build-up to make the weight. On raceday he was tempted by a seafood stand. All White was going well to Becher's on the second circuit when Williams pulled him up and was violently sick. He then rejoined the race to finish eighth to Poethlyn, with Ernie Piggott up.

In 1921 the owner of fourth-placed Turkey Buzzard, Mrs.Hollins, thought her jockey Capt. Bennet, who had remounted three times to come fourth, had been unduly hard on her horse and chased him round the paddock with her umbrella.

The second-placed rider, Harry Brown, remounted The Boredespitea with a broken collar bone, while also in that race an American, Morgan D. Blair, fell from his own Bonnie Charlie four times before retiring from the fray.

By 1922, after several years of carnage, modifications to the conditions were being mooted, with the RSPCA taking an interest.

Doubling the entry fee only succeeded in putting up the prize fund, so this hardly put off entrants in 1923. The race was won for the first time by an American owner, Stephen Sanford, whose father John, a carpet magnate, bought him the horse as a present. Sergeant Murphy was ridden by Captain Geoffrey 'Tuppy'Bennet, a qualified vet, who the following day won the first ever Foxhunters' - a full National distance in those days - on Gracious. He died after a December fall at Wolverhampton in January 1924 without regaining consciousness. Crash helmets became compulsory after this.

1924 winning horse Master Robert was so useless on the Flat in Ireland that he became a plough horse in Donegal. He was bought by Lord Airlie who won a race on him in 1922, putting up 37lbs overweight. Master Robert's National rider Robert Trudgill had cut his leg badly in a fall the previous day, but insisted on taking the ride, with the wound newly stitched. In the winner's enclosure afterwards, blood was seen pouring from the leg.

Olympic links

Right:
Olympian Harry
Llewellyn on
Foxhunter

In the equestrian world it is quite unusual, surprisingly, for riders to swap disciplines. Three-day eventers have to do some dressage and show jumping as part of their sport, but seldom to the level needed when they are individual sports. Also, in the past eventing also included a steeplechase phase, but this was done individually against the clock and much slower than racing. Top show jumper Nick Skelton had wanted to be a jockey, but the scales put paid to that. However one of jump racing's greatest protagonists, John Francome, represented Great Britain at Junior level in show jumping. Amateur jockey Chris Collins, who managed a third place in the Grand National progressed to eventing and was a mainstay of British teams in the seventies, but never achieved his ambition of making the Olympics.

There are two riders, however, who have both ridden in the Grand National and ridden for their countries at the Olympics. The first was Harry Llewellyn, born in 1911, a Welsh baronet, who won over 60 races over fences. He, like many an amateur before and after, had a continual and increasing battle with the scales, and was all set to hang up his boots when he took a liking to a chestnut gelding of his father's, Ego. It was in 1935 when the horse was eight years old that Harry decided to have a go at the National, and in 1936, having lost three and a half stone, he piloted Ego into second place twelve lengths behind Reynoldstown under fellow amateur Fulke Walwyn. The

following year they were fourth.

After the War, where he had become a Lieutenant Colonel, he was part of the British Show Jumping team on Foxhunter at the 1948 London Olympics, winning a team bronze. At the 1952 Olympics at Helsinki he partnered the same horse, and being the last to go, jumped a perfect clear round to win Britain's first ever gold medal for show jumping. The pair were a mainstay of British teams and were in 12 winning Nations Cup setups.

Eddie Harty, born in Dublin in 1937, started off show jumping, but was riding in hurdle races from the age of 14, and won many point-to-points. He then went to America to become a cowboy for a couple of years. Returning to race riding he first rode as an amateur in the National in 1960, falling at the first Becher's. That year he was selected as a member of the Irish three-day eventing team for the Rome Olympics

in 1960 where he was individual ninth on Harlequin. He then became a professional jockey and in 1969, while riding as a substitute for the injured Owen McNally, he rode the Toby Balding-trained Highland Wedding to a decisive twelve lengths win in the National. His brother John was 18th in the Eventing at the 1964 Tokyo Olympics with San Michele, before going on to win the Irish National in 1980 on Daletta.

Left:
Eddie Harty led in on Highland Wedding 1969

Facts in History

Jockey toughness: *Three time champion Jockey Terry Biddlecombe, whose eleven rides in the National only provided one runner-up spot, fractured his collarbone eight times, arms five times, shoulder blades, vertebrae, ribs, wrists, fingers, thumbs and a leg leg. He also badly bruised his kidneys being dragged 200 yards with his foot aught in a stirrup. One magazine ran a photo of a posed smiling jockey in his silks , pointing arrows at all his injury spots.*

Facts in History

A traditional way of naming a racehorse is to take part of the sire's name and mash it with the dam's name. One Grand National horse was out of a mare called Mared by a sire called Quorum.

1925 saw the first use of a taped start.

Mr. Bill Whitbread rode his own Ben Cruchan in the 1925 race. They failed to complete, but Whitbread would later pioneer race sponsorship with the Whitbread Gold Cup, and indeed also the Badminton Horse Trials.

The 1926 race saw Tasmanian jockey William Watkinson, who had been second in 1922 on Driftercome in ahead of the field on the American hope, Jack Horner. Sadly the rider was killed in a fall at Bogside only three weeks after his triumph.

The Grand National was first broadcast on the radio in 1927. A misty day, the commentators, Meyrick Good and George Allison, had their work cut out as the field was the largest there had yet been at 37 starters.

The favourite in 1927 was Sprig, who had been fourth twice. He was owned by Mrs. Mary Partridge, whose son Richard had bred him while on leave from the trenches in the Great War, with the ambition of riding him at Aintree. Sadly he was killed just weeks before the end of the war and the horse's career became a memorial to the son. Sent to the father-and-son training and riding yard of Tom and Ted Leader, who just as much wanted the horse to win for the grieving mother, Sprig came in ahead of 100-1 outsider, Bovril III.

A bigger field yet in 1928 of 42 starters produced only two finishers. The winner was Tipperary Tim, ridden by a Chester solicitor William (Bill) Dutton, followed home by the remounted Billy Barton and Tommy Cullinan.

Sixty six starters lined up in two packs in the 1929 running, with 56 failing to finish. The winning rider was Australian Robert Everett aboard Gregalach. He had previously ridden in South Africa.

Below:
Old Becher's 1920s

Bill Davies

William (Bill) Davies bought Aintree from Mirabel Topham in 1973. Davies was then a 39 year old local property developer, who, though somewhat demonised during his ownership, was keen enough on the tradition that he bought himself a runner for the 1974 race, a seven year- old called Wolverhampton. It was pulled up that year and dropped dead in training in 1975. Davies' ownership of the course was not a happy time for either him or the race itself and he endured several run-ins with the Jockey Club. He had grand ambitions, not least to reintroduce motor racing and run an Aintree Derby. None of these came to fruition. The Grand National was going through uncertain times. In 1975 Davies said he was selling Aintree to an Irish developer, Patrick McCrea, but the deal fell through. The Jockey Club threatened to move the race to Doncaster or Haydock. Ladbrokes came to the rescue and leased the course from Davies for seven years. The deal was to end in 1982 and then the future of the race was up in the air again. Davies was now asking £7 million for the course, which was more than the Levy Board would pay. A public appeal was launched but failed to reach sufficient funds. In 1983 the race was able to be run when a subsidiary of the Jockey Club, the Racecourse Holdings Trust, put up a quarter of a million pounds to put it on, and another quarter of a million for an option to buy the course for £4 million pounds. Canadian drinks company Seagram came to the rescue in 1984 with a five year sponsorship deal and an extra five year option. Davies eventually settled for a sum of £3,400,000 and the course passed into the hands of the Jockey Club.

Left:
Bill Davies with Mrs. Mirabel Topham

Facts in History

In 1930 jockey Tommy Cullinan lost both his stirrups at the second last when well up on Shaun Goilin, conceding the lead to Melleray's Belle and J.Mason, who also lost an iron. Shaun Goilin eventually prevailed, with third-placed Sir Lindsay's rider Dudley Williams also stirrup-less - so that the first three jockeys home had just one pedal between them.

The runners in 1935 included a horse, Jimmy James, owned by circus promoter Bertram Mills, but the race was won by Frank Furlong on his father's owned and trained Reynoldstown. Thus the headlines read: "Grand National won by two Furlongs". Frank was the second Old Harrovian to win the race after John Maunsell Richardson in 1873.

Fulke Walwyn, taking the place of his good friend Frank Furlong, who could not make the weight this time, won in 1936 riding the previous year's victor Reynoldstown. Coming to the second last, outsider Davy Jones was in the lead with Anthony Mildmay up, but pecked heavily and the rein buckle broke, letting the combination run out to the left of the final obstacle.

Sixteen year-old Bruce Hobbs fell with Flying Minutes on his debut in 1937 but one year later won it on the tiny 15.2hh Battleship. The trainer, Hobbs' father Reg, thought that the horse would land on his nose after the drop fences, so had the reins lengthened by 18 inches. At the fence before the Canal Turn, Hobbs was nearly unseated when Battleship veered left to the next jump. Fellow jockey Fred Rimell, alongside, sportingly pulled Bruce back into the saddle. The trainer was right about the horse's nose contact with the ground. What was first thought of as a burst blood vessel was actually a cut from nose-diving.

The winning rider in 1939, Tim Hyde (on Workman), was a successful show jumper, whom the trainer, Jack Ruttle, persuaded to become a jump jockey.

In 1940 several serving jockeys were given leave to ride in the race. The winning rider on Bogskar was Flight Sergeant Mervyn Jones. Racegoers were given air raid instructions.

Tim Durant

Tim Durant was the oldest rider to complete the Grand National, at the age of 68, in 1968 on his own horse Highlandie. It was his third attempt. He remounted after falling at the second Becher's and came in 15th of the 17 finishers. Durant was a Yale graduate in Russian literature, wanted to be a millionaire by the age of 30 and helped his cause by marrying into a very rich family.

However he lost all his money (and subsequently his wife) after the Wall Street Crash of 1929. He then went to Hollywood and became a stunt rider in Westerns. He became a friend of film director John Huston, at whose home in Ireland he remarried. It was only at the age of sixty that he decided he wanted to ride in the Grand National, and he proved his fitness by riding in a marathon trek over the Sierra Nevada. His married daughter financially supported this folly and he bought a Foxhunters winner, Ariel III.

He rode round Aintree in the Becher Chase, but Ariel couldn't run in 1966 because of tendon trouble. His daughter then bought him a replacement, King Pin. They got round two thirds of the track, but the horse had to be put down after a fall in Sweden. Durant was then diagnosed with bone cancer and it seemed he might have to have a leg amputated. After a second opinion his leg was saved, and Ariel was now fit again.

Durant wouldn't carry a whip however, and had he done so might have got farther than the 19th in Foinavon's year, 1967, before making it the next year.

Facts in History

From 1941 to 1945 there was no Grand National and Aintree became home to American troops. Mirabel Topham took over chairmanship of the Aintree Company from her husband Ronald after World War II and got Aintree raceready just weeks after troops had left the premises.

A crowd of almost 300,000 people came to watchthe first postwar race in 1946. The winning rider in 1946, top amateur Capt. Robert Petre who steered Lovely Cottage to victory, survived the War and race riding only to have his leg amputated after a slip on a breakwater.

Major Skrine, who wanted to ride his own Martin M in 1947, had one of his legs surgically shortened to match the one that had been injured in the war. He remounted in the race to finish an honourable 12th.

Despite the introduction of photo finishes in 1947 there has never been a dead heat in the Grand National.

There have been several delayed starts to the race. Indeed, the very first running in 1839 started two hours late at three o'clock. There were many false starts and in 1857 they only got off at the eighth try.

In 1858 snow postponed the run from Wednesday to Saturday. Starting tapes were introduced in 1925 which improved matters, but there have been other delays over the years. In 2005 the race was put back by 25 minutes to accommodate Prince Charles' wedding to Camilla Parker Bowles, whose former husband Andrew had ridden in the race. The wedding had to be re-arranged as the Pope had died that week.

1948 winner Sheila's Cottage was a very bad-tempered mare. At a photo shoot on the Monday after the race she bit the tip off the finger of her jockey Arthur Thompson. Lord Sefton sold the racecourse to Tophams Ltd. in 1949. This was also the first year of the one-circuit (18 fences) Topham Trophy.

1949 was the last year that the amateur Grand National, the Foxhunters', was run over the full National course.

Aristo riders: *Lord Mildmay was third in the 1948 Grand National fourth in 1949, both times on his own horse Cromwell.*

The 1951 race had a shambolic start with jockeys not ready and, in the scramble to get going, 12 fell at the first. Only three finished, one a remount.

In 1952 the Topham family had a row with the BBC with the result that Mrs. Topham put her own team in to commentate on the radio. It was an embarrassing disaster. Her amateur chums even called the eventual winner, Teal, a faller at the first.

Aristo riders: *Spanish nobleman the Duke of Aurquerque fell with Brown Jack III in 1952, and the Marquis de Portago pulled up Icy Calm.*

Facts in History

In 1953 a less than politically correctly named horse, Little Yid, was in the line-up.

Irish Lizard won the Topham in 1953 and two days later came third in the National.

Four horses - Dominick's Bar, Paris New York, Legal Joy, and Coneyburrow - were killed in the 1954 race.

In 1955 the race was nearly cancelled due to waterlogging. It went ahead but the water jump was bypassed.

A motor racing track was built inside the course in 1955 which subsequently hosted the British Grand Prix. The track became a major factor in the ability to televise the race.

Jockey Gerry Scott had broken his collarbone for the second time in five days just a week before the 1960 race. Determined to ride the favourite, he was strapped up and steered Merryman II to victory.

1961 saw sponsorship from Schweppes and the Irish Hospital Sweepstake.

The 1961 winning rider on Nicolaus Silver was Bobby Beasley, whose grandfather Harry had won the race in 1891 on Come Away.

In 1963, after 11 years of absence, the Duke of Alburquerque came back for another go, only to fall again.

The 1963 winner, Ayala, cost Lester Piggott's father Keith only £200 at Epsom, and was owned by society hairdresser Pierre 'Teazy Weazy' Raymond.

Aristo riders: *Lord Oaksey (as Mr. John Lawrence) came second in 1963 on Carrickbeg.*

Just before the 1964 race a light plane crashed by the Canal Turn killing all five passengers, who were guests of Mrs. Topham. Among these was the broadcaster and journalist Nancy Spain, due to commentate on the National.

The Course

Below:
*Over the first,
heading for Bechers
at the top*

There are 30 obstacles to be jumped on the Grand National course, with contestants going almost twice round the left-handed track, jumping all but two fences - The Chair and the Water Jump -

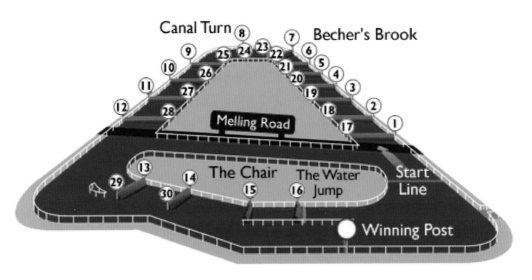

Above:
Course map

twice. These two obstacles are in front of the grandstands alongside the run in to the finishing post. The distance is about 4 miles 856 yards.

Aintree fences are unique in their appearance. Unlike jumps on the usual park courses and point-to-points, which are made of stiff birch brush, at the Grand National there is an under-structure, greatly modified over the years, but dressed with green spruce. From the landing side they resemble conifer walls. Since 1961 there has been a sloping "apron" on the take-off side which allows for a rather less daunting approach. They were made even more sloping in 2001. The minimum height is 4'6" apart from the Water.

Fence 1 (17): A scene of annual mayhem as there are over 400 yards and a crossing of the Melling Road from the start to the first fence. Riders are jostling for position and despite entreaties to take a pull, often approach too fast. Recently the distance from start to first has been slightly reduced to make for a less frenetic gallop but the hazard still exists. There are six fences down the longest straight on the course, which is mildly downhill. Among previous winners to fall at the first are the fairy tale winner of the previous year, Aldaniti; Hallo Dandy; Ayala; Gay Trip and even Gold Cup hero, Golden Miller. In 1951 many horses were facing the wrong way when the tape came down, so there was an unseemly rush to make up time. Twelve crashed out. Oddly the biggest field of 66 all cleared it in 1929. In 1999 the fence was made a couple of

yards wider to reduce bunching.

Fence 2 (18): At 4'7" this is another plain fence which has caused little problem, except for the mare FAN, after whom it was (briefly) named, and Freebooter, who won in 1950 only to be brought down by a loose horse the next year after the debacle at the first.

Fence 3 (19): This is the first open ditch, 5ft high and 6ft wide, with a bit of a drop on landing. This is another early jump that can cut the numbers down quite dramatically. Eight of 28 came down here in 1970.

Fence 4 (20): Plain fence, 4'10"

Fence 5 (21): Plain fence, 5 ft. This is the one before Becher's. From the take-off side, the fences which are not open ditches look much the same, but for many years Becher's has been signalled by a hedge on the inside track.

Fence 6 (22): Becher's Brook, the most famous steeplechase fence in the world. 4'10" on the take-off side

Above:
First fence mayhem

there was a 5'6" drop on landing over a gaping ditch. In 1990 most of the risk of landing in the V shaped ditch was removed when the lip was levelled and the brook covered over. It was a cosmetic move which may have reduced one or two accidents, but very much compromised the spectacular look of the jump and in turn the kudos of jumping it well. There is still a slightly bigger drop on the 'brave man's' inside route. Taken on the outside it feels as if you are jumping into the crowd because the course swings slightly to the left on landing.

Fence 7 (23): This small jump is meant to be a let up after Becher's but as such can be taken too casually. It became infamous in 1967 when a loose horse took out most of the field on the second circuit, enabling 100-1 chance Foinavon through under John Buckingham. The fence has since been known as Foinavon.

Fence 8 (24): The Canal Turn. This is a most unusual racing obstacle which stands at 5 ft. It was once another open ditch too. On landing, riders have to turn ninety degrees left. Early runners who failed to make the turn could end up in the Leeds Liverpool Canal. There is often bunching on the inside as many lengths can be lost here. So much spruce is kicked out that "tail-end Charlies" have quite a small fence to pop over.

Fence 9 (25): This comes up more quickly than any fence on the

course, especially considering the turn. The first of four down the other, shorter long side of what is almost a triangular course, it is 5ft high on take-off but like Becher's, has a drop and the same brook on landing. Also like Becher's it

Above:
Trouble
at Bechers

57

is named after an early incident (though Capt. Becher fell there too) and is now known as Valentine's.

Fence 10 (26): This is a 5ft high plain fence which sometimes heralds the end for tiring horses on the final circuit, as do the next two.

Fence 11 (27): A bit like the third, 5ft high with a 6ft gaping open ditch in front, but horses are into their stride by the time they meet it first time round. Not without trouble though, a Foinavon-type

incident happened in1932 when a loose horse took out two thirds of the field. Golden Miller refused to jump it on the first circuit the year after winning the race and it saw the end of first lady rider Charlotte Brew's attempt on the second circuit in 1977.

Fence 12 (28): The last before the second crossing of the Melling Road, approaching Anchor Bridge, is another five-footer, with an unseen ditch on landing. There is now a long

gallop until they join what is known as 'the racecourse proper.'

Fence 13 (29): A plain fence, 4'7"; the first in the Topham and Foxhunters', which in those races has its share of fallers.

Fence 14 (30): Innocuous enough on the first circuit at 4'6" it comes into its own as one of the most photographed next time round as it is the final jump before the long run in.

Fence 15: The biggest fence on the course, at 5'2" with a 6ft gaping ditch, is the Chair. The landing sometimes catches riders out as it is higher than the take-off, and uncomfortable jumpers can peck on landing and shoot their jockeys into orbit.

Fence 16: The water jump is only 2'6" high, but has a shallow water spread of 12'6". It seldom causes trouble, but is on the site of what was once a solid stone wall. There is another long trek back across the Melling Road and they do it all over again.

The distance from the last fence to the finishing post is a very long 494 yards. Halfway up this the course jinks to the right, when on the first circuit horses would have gone straight on to tackle the Chair and the Water Jump. Several horses have lost valuable rhythm by hanging left as if to go straight on. This kink is known as the Elbow.

Facts in History

In 1964 Mrs. Topham announced she was selling the racecourse to property developers Capital and Counties Property Ltd. Previous owner Lord Sefton objected, saying this contravened the terms of sale that the property would retain racing. In a messy outcome, the Tophams had control, as it was they who ran the race. 1965 was set to be the last Grand National.

Negotiations stalled, so there was to be a 1966 race.

The Grand National in 1965 was won by American amateur Tommy Smith on Jay Trump. Third that year was perfume entrepreneur and amateur jockey Mr. Chris Collins on Mr. Jones. He would become an international Event rider.

Right:
Nicolaus Silver in
1961. Only the
second grey after The
Lamb to win

Far Right:
Jockey and journalist
Lord Oaksey

The winning jockey of 1966, Tim Norman, on Anglo, was injured in a car crash on the way to the races. Stitched up, he was declared fit to ride.

The day before the notorious Foinavon National of 1967, a two-year-old dead-heated in a Selling Plate at Aintree. It was Red Rum.

The 1968 race was flagged up as really, really, the last ever running of the race. The owner of the favourite Different Class, who came in third, was the film star Gregory Peck who described the race as the finest sporting spectacle in the world.

Liverpool Corporation expressed an interest in saving the race in 1969 but it still fell to The Levy Board and Tophams to keep it going, which continued until 1972 when BP joined the sponsorship. Talks with the council broke down, so the race was still at risk and '72 was billed as yet another 'last' National.

Soon to retire jockey Pat Taaffe won the race in 1970 on Gay Trip, 15 years after his first win on Quare Times. Fancy!

In 1973 Mrs. Topham announced she was selling the course to property developer Bill Davies, with a none too hopeful thought that the race could continue. It was sold in November of that year for £3,000,000.

Weights/Handicapping

Handicapping is the system whereby every horse at the start is assessed on previous form and given a weight to carry accordingly. The never achievable handicapper's dream is to have a dead heat of all runners. Not all races are handicaps – some are run on level weights.

Bearing in mind how much smaller people were in the mid-1800s, the initial level weight of 12 st for the Grand National runners was relatively high and would have taken into account considerably heavier tack. The first winner Lottery, however, was forced to run under 13 st 4 lbs the following year, while all the other runners still carried 12st, on account of picking up the penalty of being 'the winner of the 1840 Cheltenham Steeplechase [who] will carry an extra 18lbs'. He still went off favourite, but under that enormous weight was pulled up exhausted on the second circuit. The same thing happened to him the next year. This was somewhat arbitrary handicapping but in 1843 it became a real handicap. The weights ranged from top of 12 st 8 lbs to bottom of 11 st. Recent winners had to take on an extra 5 lbs. Edward Topham, whose family would be involved in Aintree for over a hundred years, was the first handicapper. He raised the favourite, Peter Simple (a recent winner) to 13 st 1 lb.

The bottom weight was getting lower and lower and went from 10 st 7 lbs in 1844 down to 10 st in 1846. In 1850 The Pony was only asked to carry 8 st 7 lbs (51 lbs below the top weight). The lowest ever was in 1858,

Left:
Venetia Williams
unveils the entries
weights and odds,
Feb 2010

when Conrad came fifth under 8 st 4 lbs. Even the slightest jump jockey today would fail to get close to this. Times and results in those early days become meaningless to statisticians.

Until 1952 there was a quite a long period when the top weight was 12 st 7 lbs. From then on, top weight was 12 st, only exceeded by a pound in 1956 on third-placed Royal Tan. The minimum weight set itself at 10 st in 1937.

The handicapper doesn't have to spread the weights between the established top and bottom weights and if a big favourite pulls out the weights can concertina. This happened in 1965 when favourite Mill House pulled out, and 36 of the 47 runners ran on the minimum weight of 10 st 13 lbs.

The handicapper for the Grand National takes an annual one-off removal from his deliberations of 'park' course form, when Aintree experience colours his decisions.

Facts in History

In 1973, Red Rum came to the rescue and re-ignited public interest with his mighty overhaul of the gallant Crisp on the line. He won it again in 1974, was beaten by L'Escargot in '75 and Rag Trade in '76, but won a record third National in '77.

In 1974 Bill Davies ran the race through his Walton Group, put up some extra prize money and even bought a horse to run in the race, showing some commitment to the continuation. The Tophams kept a link by donating a trophy to the winning owner. In 1975 property prices were dropping and he was forced to put up admission charges. The 1975 crowd was the smallest on record.

The Duke of Alburquerque rode again in 1974 on Nereo to come eighth.

Singer Dorothy Squires owned tenth-placed runner Norwegian Flag in 1974.

Vincent O'Brien, though subsequently better known as one of the finest Flat trainers of all time, won a hat-trick of Nationals between 1953 and 1955 with Early Mist, Royal Tan and Quare Times.

1977 saw the first lady rider in the race. Charlotte Brew, who had been the first of her sex to complete one circuit of the course, coming fourth in the Foxhunters' the previous year, ran Barony Fort in the real thing. They ground to a halt four from home. The gallant Duke of Alburquerque was stood down on medical orders from riding his Nereo in 1977.

The race was sponsored by The Colt Car Company in 1979. They since became long-time sponsors of the Mitsubishi Motors Badminton Horse Trials.

Two sports stars had runners in the 1979 race. Liverpool footballer Emlyn Hughes had Wayward Scot, co-owned with Ginger McCain, Red Rum's trainer. He fell. Former British Lion rugby player, John Douglas, had Rubstic in the race with Maurice Barnes up. He won.

Below:
Pat Taaffe
and Gay Trip

Fred Rimell

Right:
Fred Rimell

Rimell was one of the great Aintree protagonists of the twentieth century. His family were into all the country pursuits of hunting, shooting and fishing, and he started working for his trainer father Tom at the age of twelve. His first win in a flat race was on a father trained, grandfather owned horse called Rolie.

Aged 18 he went to Aintree to help his father saddle up Forbra in 1932. He was deemed not yet experienced enough to take the ride and Tim Hamey was put up. They won at 50-1, so father Rimell was somewhat vindicated. Like several jockeys, Fred started his riding career on the Flat, winning 34 races but, as so often happens, the scales beat him and he changed codes to the jumps. His first of four championships came in the 1938/39 season. He won it again the next year.

Fred's first taste of the big race was inauspicious however. In 1936 he was riding the favourite, Avenger, who was trained by his father. He was 23 years old. At the first fence second time round the horse made a complete hash of it and fell fatally with a broken neck. The following year he fell with Delachance, managed twelfth with Provocative in 1938, but then fell again in 1939 and 1940 from Teme Willow and Black Hawk, before the War put paid to the Grand National for its duration.

Fred broke his neck (the second time that year) in the 1947 Cheltenham Gold Cup and had to hang up his riding boots. He was

Above:
Fred Rimell leads
in Gay Trip 1970

in plaster for eight months. He was never to win a race at Cheltenham or Liverpool, his best possible chance having been Forbra when he didn't get the winning ride.

Fred had started training after the war, while he was still riding, more than ably assisted by his wife Mercy, whom he had met in the hunting field. He now took up handling full time and had a stellar career from his Kinnersley yard in Worcestershire. He won two Gold Cups (Woodland Venture and Royal Frolic), two Champion Hurdles (Comedy of Errors, twice) and many other big races. He was champion trainer five times, to add to his four as a jockey. It would be the Grand National however where he remained the sole record holder of four wins as a trainer.

His first win has perhaps gone down somewhat unfairly as a fluke as ESB took the1956 race ahead of the bizarrely spread eagled Devon Loch close to the finishing post. His next success was with Nicolaus Silver in 1961, beating the previous year's winner Merryman II. Greys are popular winners with the public but he was only the second ever, the first being 90 years before,when The Lamb was, literally, the dream winner.

Gay Trip then won by 20 lengths in 1970. This was a considerable feat, as the horse had never won a race longer than two-and-a-half miles and was carrying top weight. He was piloted by Pat Taaffe, a top jockey most associated with the great Arkle. The following year, the horse was one of several former and later winners to be first-fence fallers on their return to the course.

In 1976 Rimell took on the training of Rag Trade, a finisher the previous year. He won by two lengths from Red Rum during one of the great eras of Grand National history.

Though Rimell sent out four runners for the next four Nationals, he never won the race again, despite several placings. His record was eventually to be shared by Ginger McCain, after the other Aintree specialist proved that Red Rum was not his only winner when Amberleigh House came in.

Broadcasting

The first radio broadcast of the race was in 1927 by the BBC. The commentators were a journalist from The Sporting Life magazine, Meyrick Good, and news journalist, George Allison. Allison did all the pre and post-race 'colour' pieces and anchored the programme until 1934, when in a bizarre career move he became manager of Arsenal Football Club. (The mind boggles to imagine Arsene Wenger calling a National). With no commentary box, Meyrick broadcast with a mouth microphone and a second to capture crowd cheers in a seat in the stand sitting next to King George V. How he managed at all on such a misty day is greatly to his credit. Obviously unable to see all the action he nevertheless kept up the spirit and in the final strides became very excited when Sprig, the favourite, came in. He had backed him and was a lifelong friend of the trainer, Tom Leader. The whole broadcast was deemed a great success and ran for an hour.

The race was first televised in 1960 with commentators Peter O'Sullevan, Peter Dimmock and another newspaper man, Clive Graham. The front man was Cliff Michelmore, standing in for

by a tap on the shoulder mid-commentary by earlier-decanted champion jockey, Fred Winter, who had climbed up to watch the remainder of the race.

The five year old motor racing track inside the race course was perfect for tracking cameras to follow the race. The once a year audiences began to identify more with the commentary voices, not least the Irish tones of Michael O'Hehir, who unforgettably described the mayhem at the fence after Becher's in the 1967 Foinavon year.

Another classic handover for many years was the O'Sullevan line, "And, as they cross the Melling Road, it's over to John Hanmer."

1969 was the first year of colour transmission which, for those who had the sets, made following the race that much easier. Coleman was now well installed as anchor. He was succeeded for 13 years by Des Lynam in 1985. Des leased a

David Coleman who was off with appendicitis. Oddly, the race was won by the favourite (Merryman II) for the first time since Sprig on the day of the first radio broadcast.

O'Sullevan started on radio and covered 50 Nationals until his retirement in 1997. In that first year of TV, Peter Dimmock, a vertigo sufferer, was installed up a scaffolding tower. He was distracted

Right:
Sue Barker

horse, Another Duke, to run in his colours in the 1986 race. He fell with future champion trainer Paul Nicholls on board.

Viewing figures in the UK had been about 16,000,000 but dropped to just over 11,000,000 in the mid-nineties, then rising to over 15,000,000 when the race was re-run on the Monday in 1997 (after a bomb scare put paid to the Saturday running). That was O'Sullevan's last year as lead race reader and he handed over to Australian Jim McGrath, who had been part of the team for several years.

Over the years the build-up to the race has been expertly covered, with recorded stable visits and helicopter flights round the course. On one or two occasions riders from other disciplines, such as Mark Phillips from eventing and Harvey Smith from show jumping, joined old pros like Richard Pitman to have a filmed spin round the

course, while miked up.

In 2000 Sue Barker and Clare Balding took over fronting the programme from Des Lynam.

Home viewing figures for all programmes have declined with the introduction of multiple channels but the race is still seen by an estimated 600 million worldwide.

From 2013 the BBC stopped covering horse racing and the mantle moved to Channel 4.

Foinavon

The day before the 1967 National, Foinavon was a 500-1 outsider and neither his owner nor trainer turned up to watch him run. On the day he started at 100-1. His chances were described by Clive Graham, in the Daily Express, thus: 'Not the boldest of jumpers; he can be safely ignored, even in a race noted for shocks'.

The race was running without much incident, and indeed 30 of the 44 starters were still clear at Becher's on the second circuit. The next fence, at 4' 6" is the smallest on the course. A first fence faller, Popham Down, was still leading the field and on the inside. At the 23rd, for no apparent reason he baulked to the right and ran along the fence, taking out almost the entire field of following contenders. There was

chaos, with jockeys trying to catch their horses, second attempts at the fence and now many more loose horses. From the safety of a hundred-yard deficit behind the leaders, Foinavon cantered into contention under John Buckingham. Seeing the carnage, the jockey steered to the outside and popped the jump almost from a standstill. They were the only combination to clear it at first time of asking. Sixteen others reconvened, including Josh Gifford on the runner-up and favourite

Above:
The Foinavon
pile up 1967

Right:
*Foinavon comes in
at 100-1 under John
Buckingham*

Honey End, who took a 50 yard run-up for his second attempt. Foinavon won by 15 lengths and the Tote paid out on a record 444-1.

The trainer, John Kempton, was himself riding at Worcester on National day (he would have put up 10 lbs overweight had he ridden Foinavon) so his father Jack saddled the horse. It was jockey John Buckingham's first attempt and owner, Cyril Watkins watched the race on TV but had to go out of the room as events unfolded.

The horse was actually named by Anne, Duchess of Westminster, for whom he had been bought originally by her trainer Tom Dreaper. Like her famous Arkle, Foinavon was named after a Scottish mountain.

Three days before the 1967 National, John Buckingham, about to go to an uncle's funeral was booked to ride Foinavon because of his rider/trainer's difficulty with the scales. Three other jockeys had turned down the dubious chance as the owner was only prepared to pay the standard fee of £5-10s, when most owners paid a National premium. The night before the race the 26 year old jockey slept on two pushed together chairs in a Liverpool boarding house. Two nights later he was appearing on stage and TV with host Bob Monkhouse in *Sunday Night at the London Palladium.*

The Foinavon victory has been derided as a fluke but the winning time was average and Buckingham completed all four Nationals he contested. He had never sat on a horse until leaving school at 15. His mother worked as a dairymaid on Edward Courage's estate and John had the chance of being assistant shepherd, gamekeeper or stable lad. He remained in racing till his retirement, working as a very popular jockey's valet for 30 years.

Facts in History

The 1979 Gold Cup winner Alverton, ridden by Jonjo O'Neill, was killed in a fall at Becher's. In 1979 nine horses went out of the race at the Chair.

Timber racing specialist Ben Nevis won the 1980 race under American merchant banking rider Charlie Fenwick. His less-than-welcome encouragement on leaving the paddock was: 'Keep on remounting.'

1981 Aldaniti and Bob Champion won from amateur John Thorne on Spartan Missile. John's son Nigel had been killed in a car crash shortly after his first National ride in 1968. John was killed in a point-to-point accident a year later.

By 1982, the last year of Ladbrokes' administration, owner Bill Davies had put the price of the course up to £7,000,000, somewhat more than the £400,000 he had been offered not-many years before. The Jockey Club entered negotiations, but basically the race was to be saved by public subscription. There were just seven months to raise the seven million pounds. By the end of 1982 the sum had not been raisedbut they

went to Davies with an offer of £4,000,000. More fundraising was needed and with the help of the County Council of Merseyside an appeal was chaired by Lord Vestey. A bit more time was bought. In 1984 the whisky firm Seagram saved the race as sponsors and Davies accepted the Jockey Club's offer of £3,400,000, into whose ownership it would fall. The National was saved.

The 1982 race was won by 48-year-old amateur Dick Saunders on Grittar.

The first lady to complete the race was Geraldine Rees, a former three-day eventer, in 1982 on Cheers. Charlotte Brew was also a contender who was unseated from Martinstown.

1983 saw the first winning female trainer when Corbiere came in for Jenny Pitman with Ben de Haan up. Geraldine Rees and American Mrs. Joy Carrier were in the race, but failed to complete.

Left:
*Victorious amateur
Dick Saunders and
Grittar*

Fred Winter

Fred's father, Fred senior, had won the 1911 Oaks as a 16-year-old apprentice on Cherimoya. Young Fred was bred for the job. He went to school with Dave Dick at Ewell Castle School. They were both destined to ride National winners.

Just before the War, 13 year old Fred started riding and winning Flat races. His first was Tam O'Shanter for his father at Salisbury. The usual story of the dratted scales headed Fred to jump racing, but not before he did his national service in the Parachute Regiment.

Back from the army he set about becoming a jump jockey, but early on fractured his spine and was out for a year. He then went to work for Capt. Ryan Price, where he remained for 16 years.

Fred's first ride in the National was in 1951 on Glen Fire. Eleven came down at the first that year, but they avoided the aftermath and lasted as long as the first Canal Turn.

Although Fred was Champion Jockey for 1952/53 he suffered a broken leg in 1954 and his next National ride wasn't until 1955, when he fell from Oriental Way at the 11th. His next ride Sundew crashed out at Becher's in the Devon Loch year. However, horse and rider came back to win in 1957.

Winter's next three Nationals ended up with him on the deck, then he came fifth on Kilmore. Next season, though he was retained by Fulke Walwyn, he kept the Ryan Price-trained ride on Kilmore in the National. He jumped into the lead at the final fence and went onto

win by ten lengths.

In 1964 he took over the disused Uplands yard in Upper Lambourn. The following year, in his first season he trained American owned, bred and ridden Jay Trump to win the National under amateur Tommy Smith. The trainer repeated the feat a year later with Anglo, who won by twenty lengths.

His later 70s jockeys included two of the best never to win a National: Richard Pitman, who came so agonisingly close with Crisp in Red Rum's first year, and John Francome. He also set his long-time assistant trainer, Nicky Henderson, on the road to future glories.

Cheating and Interference

The greatest steeplechase in the world is also the biggest betting race in the world. From its very first running, it has been a platform for big wagers so a certain amount of skulduggery over the years has been inevitable. In that very first race in 1839, a well-fancied Irish horse, Rust, was showing well, when a mob with an interest in him failing to win stormed the course and surrounded him until the rest of the field had passed. This happened on a narrow stretch of the course which was an optional route and so reasonably easy to pull off.

Three years later, a gang of yobs ran on to the course and hampered leader Peter Simple after Valentine's on the second circuit. His rider Mr. Hunter was unseated, but he remounted to finish third. Rust's jockey William McDonough had more trouble in 1846 when a mounted spectator crashed into him and his ride Lancet, knocking the rider off.

Rumours of 'nobbling' were rife and the following year Brunette, the mount of William's brother Alan, was thought to have been got at. She did however manage sixth place. The 1854 favourite, Miss Mowbray, had certainly been tampered with. The mare had been 'blistered' with inflammatory ointment and had to be withdrawn an hour before the race.

Much of this rigging of the

market was done by way of anonymous threats.

In 1885, second favourite and previous winner for Count Kinsky, Zoedone, had been threatened with being 'stopped' by unsigned letter. Kinsky hired detectives to make sure all feed and water was tested, but prior to the race there was a bit of a delay before the Count mounted, and he noticed a dab of blood on his white jacket, then a puncture wound in the horse's nostril. The deed had seemingly

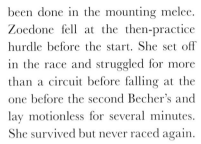

been done in the mounting melee. Zoedone fell at the then-practice hurdle before the start. She set off in the race and struggled for more than a circuit before falling at the one before the second Becher's and lay motionless for several minutes. She survived but never raced again.

In 1894 and 1895 the hot favourite, Cloister, was withdrawn shortly before the race with 'training injuries'. Many refused to believe this coincidence, but no wrongdoing was ever proved.

It was only in 1910 that doping of steeplechase horses became illegal (it had been for some time in flat racing). No National winner has been 'done' for dope.

In 1935 jockey Gerry Wilson, who had steered Golden Miller to two Cheltenham Gold Cup victories, told his trainer Basil Briscoe that he had been offered the then very substantial sum of £3,000 to take a pull on the favourite.

He wouldn't name the party but security was put in place and the trainer slept with a shotgun under his bed. It was all unnecessary in the end, as the horse tipped off his rider at the 11th obstacle.

In 1947 100-1 shot Caughoo won the National under Irish rider Eddie Dempsey, in very foggy conditions, by a substantial 20 lengths. The runner-up, Lough Conn's jockey Daniel McCann (also Irish), accused the winner of using the fog as a shield and missing out 15 obstacles by taking a short cut. It led to fisticuffs and a subsequent court case. The accusation was dismissed by the magistrates as a drink fuelled fantasy and no action taken.

There were rumours of a major attempt to rig the race in 1961, when a third of the field was apparently going to be doped. There was no proof that anything untoward had taken place, but still food for thought for conspiracy theorists. Trainer Fred Rimell, however, took no chances and swapped his two grey runners' stables. His second string, High Spot, was put in the favourite Nicolaus Silver's stall, had a bad race and never ran again. Had he been got at in error? The race was won by Nicolaus Silver, whose jockey Bobby Beasley was threatened by letter the following year not to win, but the heavy going reduced them to seventh in any case.

1998 winning rider on Earth Summit, Carl Llewellyn, told how, a year later that he had received a mobile call claiming he could become 'a very rich man' if he failed to win on the favourite. He ignored the treatise as a crank call.

In reality the National is such an unpredictable race anyway, where 'sure things' are seldom so and fluke results are the norm, that it is probably the most silly sporting event in the world to try and influence with foul play.

Ginger McCain

Very much a local to Aintree, Donald McCain was born only 15 miles from the racecourse in 1930 at Southport. A natural redhead, he was known as "Ginger" from an early age. He saw his first Grand National, aged nine, with his grandfather in 1940, the last running before hostilities turned Aintree into a base for American troops. He first worked with horses aged 13, driving a delivery cart, which was commonplace transport in those days. After compulsory national service in the army, McCain became a stable lad, and even got the odd ride in point-to-points, despite being a well-built 6'3".

His first real job, well-documented, was as a taxi driver and second-hand car salesman, but his interest in horses continued and he obtained a permit to train from the tiny yard behind his car showroom in Birkdale. He had his first winner in his early twenties, with San Lorenzo in a seller at Aintree in 1952.

McCain had no gallops so took his horses to work out on Southport Sands.

In 1967 Red Rum dead-heated in a five-furlong Aintree seller on the Flat, witnessed by McCain. The horse sold for 300 guineas, which was beyond the car salesman's budget.

In 1969 Ginger graduated from permit holder to a full training licence, but managed only one winner in his first year and none in his second. Some taxi passengers would rather not indulge in banter with their drivers. However, Ginger had a regular customer in retired

Liverpool businessman Noel Le Mare, by then in his eighties, and the two got talking about the dream of having a National runner. Ginger bought Glenkiln for him at Doncaster Sales for 1,000 guineas and he was entered in the 1972 National. In a potentially career-busting cock-up (not that McCain's career as a trainer was much in evidence anyway), he somehow managed to withdraw the horse in error! Amazingly Le Mare was sanguine and suggested buying a second string for 1973.

By an unbelievable coincidence Red Rum came up for sale again in August 1972, and Ginger secured him for Mr. Le Mare for 6,000 guineas at Doncaster Sales. Red Rum had had four previous trainers and little success, but somehow the unique training surface of the beach at Southport worked wonders and the horse won six of his nine starts under McCain's care. His epic win over the gallant Crisp in the 1973 National was the stuff of Aintree legend, with the tin-pot yard and aged owner taking the world's greatest steeplechase. Not only that, but they beat Golden Miller's course record by 19 seconds. Le Mare's first National purchase, Glenkiln, fell in both 1973 and 1974.

Red Rum won the 1974 race under top weight. McCain came in for criticism for over-racing his hero by bringing him out three weeks later for the Scottish National, yet he won that too.

After his five-year spectacular run with Red Rum's three wins and two seconds, Ginger had a lean spell and, inevitably was labelled a one horse wonder. In the 1979 race, Wayward Scot, a horse he co-owned with footballer Emlyn Hughes, crashed out at the first and his other runner Brown Admiral disposed of his rider at the 21st. He had no luck with his several

Left:
Red Rum with lad Billy Ellison

subsequent runners, but saw a former charge, Hallo Dandy, win for fellow northern trainer Gordon W. Richards in 1984. Such are the fortunes of horse racing.

In 1986 at least he had a finisher in Imperial Black, though his other entry Dudie fell at the third, was remounted and fell again at Becher's. His subsequent runners were way out in the betting.

Nevertheless in 1991 he invested in a 'proper' yard in Cheshire. He ran Hotplate twice in the National from there, but he was pulled up both times. His horses were coming back into the betting and in the void race of 1993 Sure Metal went off at 50-1. They were part of the cavalry which ran the race regardless but fell at the 20th.

In 1996 Ginger ran Sure Metal again, with his equally tall son Donald on board. At 200-1 they led over the first and did eventually finish, coming in 17th and last,

though it must have been a great moment for McCain junior to have completed the trip.

In 1999 the bookies didn't rate McCain's two runners Commercial Artist and Back Bar, sending them both off at 200-1. The first pulled up, the second completed to come in 14th.

In 2001, aged 70, He had two runners in Hanakham and Amberleigh House, the latter purchased for another local millionaire, John Halewood. The going was very boggy that year, with only four finishers, none of them trained by Ginger.

Later that year McCain trained Amberleigh House to win the 22-fence Becher Chase at the winter meeting, so his Grand National ambitions appeared to be alive and kicking. However the following year the handicapper gave the horse such a low weight, 9st 6lb, that 34 horses would have to drop out in order to get him a run. McCain pleaded for a rule change that would give proven Aintree winners a minimum of 10st, but to no avail, and with thirty drop-outs on the day, the horse was four short of a run. McCain understandably complained that the big trainers were entering large numbers of higher handicapped horses to please their owners, with no thought of running but effectively rigging the weights.

The year 2003 saw him enter three runners: Ackzo, Lambrini Gold and once again Amberleigh House. By this stage Donald Jnr was playing a very active role as assistant trainer, but Ginger was the licence holder. Amberleigh House was given a sensible weight of 10st 4lbs about which Ginger characteristically remarked, 'It's amazing what the threat of castration can do to a handicapper.'

Throughout the race he was running well, with the added 'charm' of a wisp of Red Rum's mane plaited into his own. Under Graham Lee he finished an honourable third. True to form Ginger remarked that, 'If he'd had a proper trainer then he'd have won.'

That might have been the closest that McCain would come to winning the great race again. However in 2004 the dreaded handicapper did connections something of a favour. Amberleigh House was only saddled with 10st 7lbs. To ecstatic scenes, he won, 31 years after Red Rum's first triumph. McCain had equalled Fred Rimell's record four National wins as a trainer. Reneging on his promise to retire if Amberleigh House won, he fancied a tilt at being outright record trainer, though it wasn't to be.

Having eventually handed over the training reins to Donald, he lived to see his son win the race in 2011 with Ballabriggs, dying in September of that year.

Red Rum

His sire was a top class miler, Quorum, out of a very tricky mare called Mared, who was an extremely difficult ride. Bred to run on the Flat he only realised 400 guineas from a lone bidder at his yearling sale and was owned first of all by big time gambler and businessman Maurice Kinsley, whose Sir Ken had been a three time winner of the Champion Hurdle. His first race, a two year old five furlong selling sprint, was oddly enough at Aintree in 1967, the day before the Foinavon debacle. He dead heated with a horse called Curlicue but failed to win any of his next 14 starts.

Red Rum was ridden twice into the money by Lester Piggott. The horse was then bought by a previous Grand National winning owner, Mrs. Lurline Brotherton, who had triumphed with Freebooter way back in 1950. Her trainer Bobby Renton, introduced the now-gelded Red Rum to jumping at his yard in Yorkshire. Renton's assistant trainer was a young Irishman named Tommy Stack, who took over the licence when Renton retired in 1971. Stack however had ambitions to be a jockey, so the yard was subsequently taken over by Anthony Gillam.

Red Rum was quite successful in his first attempts over the sticks, winning three hurdles and five' chases. But then in the euphemistic jargon of racing he became 'difficult to train', which is code for being lame a lot of the time. He had developed the foot bone ailment, pedal osteitis. He had managed a respectable fifth in the Scottish National, but was nevertheless sent to Doncaster sales in 1972.

Ginger McCain had seen Red

Rum in his 1967 seller at Aintree, just as he had started training, when he didn't bother to turn up at the auction, knowing he had insufficient funds to bid. This time, however, he had the backing of one of his taxi customers, Noel le Mare.

Since McCain's training premises didn't run to smart turf gallops, all his horses were exercised on Southport Sands. On the second day of having the horse in his yard, McCain took his new charge with his string to the beach. With a

sinking heart he realised that the lameness was still there. He had already tested his owner's loyalty by making a mess of the entry of his first potential National runner. Now he had persuaded Le Mare to part with 6,000 guineas for a hobbling horse. Ginger had no idea about the previous pedal osteitis. Taking him out of the string, he sent him paddling in the surf.

Ginger may well have been seen as a tin-pot trainer, stabling his charges behind his second-hand car showroom and supplementing his income as a minicab driver, but in one of those great twists of fate which have so often been connected with the Grand National, it was because of those restricted facilities that history was made.

It was the sea water and sand gallops that cured Red Rum of his lameness. In a large yard he would have trained on grass, remained lame and been discarded

as untrainable. Once back on the racecourse he won five chases in a row in seven weeks, one being over the longish distance of nearly three and a half miles. On that occasion the erstwhile Tommy Stack, his previous trainer, was unavailable to take the ride and Ginger put up Brian Fletcher for the first time. Fletcher had spent much of the previous year injured, so this was a great comeback. McCain had a winning stayer on his hands - and he kept faith with Fletcher.

The pair contested the 1973 Grand National 23 lbs better off than front-runner Crisp. Fletcher timed his move to perfection to record a famous win, perhaps then more famous for Crisp's honourable defeat than for Red Rum's victory win. It was only the next year that 'Rummy' began to look like a legend in the making. This time he had an extra 23 lbs to carry yet came home seven lengths clear of L'Escargot.

Right:
Red Rum
celebreates his
third win

Three weeks later the combination also took the Scottish National.

The following year, in 1975, under top weight, Red Rum came second to his great rival L'Escargot on the soft ground which didn't suit him. He ran near the back for the first circuit and Fletcher had even thought of pulling up the favourite. However the horse picked up, and was actually leading from the second Valentine's to the second last.

After that race Fletcher went public with his feelings that Red Rum had lost his sparkle and a fallout with McCain ensued. For the 1976 campaign Fletcher was replaced by McCain's original first choice jockey from years back, Tommy Stack, who had briefly trained the horse.

The 'Rummy' team of trainer McCain, jockey Fletcher, head lad Jackie Grainger, and his work rider Billy Ellison was to break up amid a certain amount of rancour.

Grainger was fired and Ellison left shortly after being promoted to head lad. Billy Beardwood became Red Rum's main carer in subsequent years.

Understandably, in 1976 the horse carried top weight for the third time, and went off as 10-1 second favourite. Several pundits agreed with Fletcher's notion that Rummy was now past his best. His warm-up races on park courses had not showed much promise, and a three times National winning rider had been 'jocked off'. As had happened the year before, Red Rum was at the rear of the field on the first circuit but, steered wide by Stack, the pair avoided casualties and found themselves in contention at the second last, when five horses jumped pretty well alongside each other. Landing just in front at the last Red Rum was overhauled by Rag Trade, who was carrying 12 lbs less but only beat

the dual winner by two lengths. In third place came Eyecatcher, ridden by none other than the deposed Brian Fletcher.

In what was becoming a pattern, Red Rum's build-up to the 1977 race was very moderate. He was 12 years old, but still was allotted top weight of 12st in a field of 42. However the sun had shone over Aintree for the meeting and the going totally suited the horse.

Seven came down at the first, another four at the third - the big open ditch - and two more at the fourth, the fast going no doubt contributing to the problems. There were more fallers at Becher's leaving Boom Docker out in front, pulling hard and, with his head up, looking a horribly difficult ride. He opened up a 40 length lead only to eventually run out of steam at the 17th.

The favourite Andy Pandy then took a 12-length lead only to crumple on landing at the second Becher's. That put Stack and Red Rum out in front earlier than they ideally wanted. However they extended their lead away from all bar Churchtown Boy, winner of the Topham Trophy two days earlier. He was just two lengths behind but not for long. Red Rum pulled away to win by all of 25 lengths to tumultuous applause.

He was entered for the 1978 race and, despite his usual poor racecourse form pre-Aintree, he had worked well at home. However the day before the race it was discovered that he had a hairline fracture in a small bone in his foot. He never raced again.

He did however lead the parade that year and for the next 15, having become a high-earning celebrity. He was eventually put down in October 1995 and is buried by the Aintree winning post at the scene of his greatest triumphs.

Left:
Red Rum wins
for the third time
in 1977 under
Tommy Stack

Lady Riders

The mould was broken in 1977 when Charlotte Brew, who had been the first girl to complete one circuit of the course in the previous year's Foxhunters', started Barony Fort. Though girls had ridden in point-to-point amateur racing for decades it was only in 1971 that the Jockey Club allowed them to ride 'under Rules' on professional racecourses - but this was only in amateur races on the Flat. Meriel Tufnell won the first all-ladies race at Kempton in 1972, therefore becoming the first lady rider to win on a 'real' racecourse. She retired in 1975, the year that women were first allowed to race against professional jockeys.

This however was still on the Flat. It was a strange prejudice. The Velka Pardubicka in Czechoslovakia is arguably an even greater challenge than the Grand National, with a twisty course over banks, drops and their own version of Becher's, the fearsome "Taxis", and over uneven going and plough, not unlike the early Nationals. In 1927 the Jockey Club was consulted about whether a female rider could take part. They had no objections. Hence Lata Brandisova was in the money three times before finally winning in 1937.

It was the 1976 Sex Discrimination Act which forced the authorities' hand. Diana Thorne (daughter of gallant amateur John Thorne - who was later to partner Spartan Missile as runner-up to Aldaniti) was the first lady winner under National Hunt Rules. An international three-day eventer, she subsequently married Nicky Henderson. Charlotte Brew got as far as the 27th on her big race debut in 1977, but the ladies' cause was not helped two years later when a former champion point-to-point rider, Jenny Hembrow, had a crashing first fence fall from Sandwilan. The pair got as far as the 19th the following year. In 1981 Linda Sheedy also got as far as the big ditch at the 19th (third fence first time round) aboard Deiopea.

The betting odds were shortening a bit. Miss Brew went off at 200-1. The next two ladies went off at 100-1, as did Charlotte on her second appearance in 1982 with Martinstown, when she was unseated at the third (so far an unlucky obstacle for the female riders). That year however Geraldine Rees started at 66-1 on Cheers and they completed, albeit a very tired eighth and last, to make history. On her return the following year she was a first fence casualty on Midday Welcome, starting at 500-1 but, at much better odds of 28-1 that year, American Joy

Left:
Gee Armatage

101

Right:
Venetia Williams

Carrier's King Spruce shed her at Becher's first time round. She had every right to be there having won the Maryland Hunt Cup twice - and the horse had won the Irish National the year before.

Joy Carrier was denied a return in 1985 when King's Spruce was 41st in the list of the now regulation 40 runners. Ironically 41 had started the year she first rode. The next challenger was Jacqui Oliver on Eamons Owen at 200-1. They parted company at The Chair. In 1988 no fewer than three girls lined up. Gee Armytage was on Gee-A, not named after her but owner/trainer G.A. Hubbard, who set off at 33-1. They pulled up at the 22nd. Future winning trainer Venetia Williams went off at 200-1 on Marcolo, who came down at Becher's, and Penny Ffitch-Heyes and Hettinger crashed out at the first.

The likelihood of a lady rider winning the National, even for such an unpredictable race, is

perhaps against them as they need to be put up on a decent horse in the first place, and chauvinism still exists. But still they kept coming. 1989 was the turn of Tarnya Davis, riding a late purchase Numerate, trained by her father Peter. In sticky going they lasted to the fence before the second Becher's.

Judy Davies had completed the course in the 1993 John Hughes Chase two days before the National, and duly lined up for the big one on Formula One. At the second attempt to start the race, the tape got entangled round her horse's neck and she never got going in what became known as 'The National that never was'. The following year Rosemary Henderson, all of 51 years of age, made a massive breakthrough, riding the 100-1 shot Fiddlers Pike. He was the family pet, owned and trained by the rider. She finished fifth of the six finishers, having safely hacked her way round, avoiding trouble, and got a well-deserved cheer from the crowd. If a 51-year-old female amateur could come fifth on a home-trained horse, anything now became possible.

It was a false dawn and it would be another 11 years before Carrie Ford lined up with Forest Gunner in 2005. They had won the previous year's Foxhunters over the fences just ten weeks after Carrie gave birth to a daughter. She only came out of retirement because Forest Gunner's professional rider Peter Buchanan

was claimed to ride another horse. They went off at 8-1, with a real chance. Mrs. Ford didn't disgrace herself, matching Rosemary Henderson's creditable fifth. The next year Nina Carberry, with the right pedigree of coming from a racing dynasty took the ride to come ninth. Nina rode again in 2010 on Character Building to be seventh (and 15th the next year) and was unseated in 2012 from Organised confusion when joined by another lady rider from Irish racing royalty, Katie Walsh, who came so close when third on Seabass. On the same horse she was 13th the next year and in the same place in 2014 on Vesper Bell. The Grand National has become less of a lottery over recent years, and the 'fairy tales' perhaps less likely, with fewer women jockeys around to take up the challenge. A non fluke win in the not too distant future is likely to come from a daughter or sister from an established racing family.

Charlotte Brew

Above:
Charlotte Brew
with Barony Fort

At the age of 20 Charlotte had become the first girl to successfully complete a circuit of the course, coming fourth in the 1976 Foxhunters Chase on Barony Fort. The next year this Benenden-educated girl from Essex lined up in the Grand National with 41 others. The media didn't give her an easy ride, despite the fact that lady riders had by now proved themselves at the very top in show jumping and the arguably more hazardous sport of three day eventing. Also for many years lady riders had been a feature of amateur steeplechasing, point-to-points. Charlotte had taken her fitness training seriously. Ladbrokes, who were now managing the race, gave her a £20.00 free bet at 500/1 against her completing. In the market this came down to 8/1.

Taking a sportingly Corinthian attitude to her following day's challenge, Charlotte is reputed to have gone out dancing and gambling the night before the race.

Riding sensibly, Charlotte and Barony Fort missed the seven fallers at the first and were still going steadily but fine by Becher's second time round. Becoming increasingly tailed off, they ground to a halt at the final ditch at twenty seven. Charlotte re-presented three more times, but to no avail. The pair had nevertheless got further than 31 other starters.

Geraldine Rees

After the trailblazing efforts of Charlotte Brew to be the first lady rider to line up in the National, it surely would not be long before a girl got to complete the course. Geraldine Wilson was the daughter of Northern trainer Capt. James Wilson. Her chosen equestrian sport was three-day eventing, at which she had excelled at junior level. She had been a member of the British team at the Junior European Championships in 1973. She never completed the two biggest events at Burghley and Badminton but rode in a couple of point-to-points before her debut under Rules in 1977.

On a chance ride, Twidale, in a novice hurdle at Carlisle, she set off on the outsider and was never headed. She then won her next two races. The former eventer then had a fall at the first jump in her debut attempt over fences. In time, Geraldine did become the leading female National Hunt rider, scoring most of her wins in hurdle races.

Wilson (under her married name Rees) suffered the usual catalogue of jockey injuries but still had three

Below:
Geraldine Rees and Cheers

more winners and found herself racing at Aintree in 1981 in the Red Rum Novices' Handicap Chase. An ambition was born to have a go at the big fences and she was all set to ride Gordon's Lad in the big race in 1982. Gordon's Lad was one of the very few Aintree challengers to have been trained on Southport sands, like Red Rum, however where the sea and sand had helped to make Red Rum sound, Gordon's Lad went lame a couple of weeks before the National. With history maybe about to be made, media interest understandably built up, and the Wilson family were very keen to keep the dream alive. They didn't have long to find a qualified and entered replacement mount.

There was only one available, a bay gelding called Cheers, who had completed the previous year in 12th and last place under Peter Scudamore. The horse went up for sale with his Aintree entry only eight days before the race. An emotional rollercoaster, so usual for a great Aintree story, began to unfold. The Wilsons were outbid at the sales and the horse was knocked down to trainer Charles Mackenzie for £8,000, in the ownership of his wife and a Mrs. Susan Shally.

It seemed the dream was over. On the Monday before the race however the owners rang the Wilsons to say that Geraldine could have the ride. Unlike Charlotte Brew, who had tasted the Aintree fences in the Foxhunters the year before her National debut, Saturday was to be Geraldines' baptism of fire. As it happened Charlotte was the only other lady rider in the field on a 100-1 outsider, her mother's Martinstown. Cheers went off at 66-1 with the rails offering 5-1 against him and his debut lady rider completing the course.

Cheers nearly dropped his jockey, rearing up in the paddock.

He then started misbehaving going down to the start and had to be led in at the back to face the starting tape. They avoided a first fence battle scene, only to be seriously bashed sideways by Coolishall at the third. Coolishall's jockey, Ron Barry, was unseated and Charlotte Brew also fell here.

To aid her 'stickability' in the saddle, Geraldine had rubbed resin into the seat of her breeches.

Cheers and Geraldine survived the first circuit intact and were actually going quite well, but then began to lose ground. After the second Becher's there were only eight still left in the race. Cheers was overtaken by Three of Diamonds and was now last and fading. A male professional rider would almost certainly have pulled up, but the crowd was behind Geraldine, and though both horse and rider finished exhausted Mrs. Rees had earned her place in the history books – such as this one.

Aldaniti and Bob Champion

Aldaniti was bred by Mr. Thomas Barron. The name derived from the first two letters of his grandchildren's names: Alistair, David, Nicola and Timothy.

He was bought unraced at Ascot Sales by Josh Gifford as a four-year-old in 1974 for 4,100 guineas. After winning a novice hurdle on his debut, with Bob Champion in the saddle, he was sold straight away to the Giffords' nearby clients, Nick and Valda Embiricos. Aldaniti was injured in 1976 and was off for a year before going chasing and finishing third in the 1977 Hennessy Cognac Gold Cup. Champion had thought the horse would one day win a National, but after the Hennessy he chipped a bone in his right hind leg and was off for another seven months.

In 1979 horse and jockey were fourth in the Cheltenham Gold Cup and second in the Scottish National. A tilt at Aintree in 1980 would have been the aim, but Bob had been diagnosed with cancer and had to watch Aldaniti break down under Richard Rowe at Sandown in November 1979. The trainer thought he would never race again. He was sent off to his owner's yard for TLC until November 1980 when he returned to the Giffords for proper training once more. Champion was race fit the same month; the Aintree dream was back on.

After a strong win at Ascot in February, the Cheltenham festival was subsequently bypassed in favour of the jockey's lifetime ambition. Allotted a fair weight of 10st 13lbs, Aldaniti frightened his connections with untidy jumps over the first two Liverpool obstacles before settling but he hit the front earlier than was ideal at the eleventh. He kept up his lead at the last but the favourite, Spartan Missile, and 54 year old amateur John Thorne, riding without stirrups- were storming up behind the front runners. Aldaniti prevailed by four lengths and entered into the fairy-tale history books. As is so often the fate in race riding, the 1981 heroes were first fence fallers the following year.

Bob Champion first rode in the

Above:
*Bob Champion
and Aldaniti
at the water*

Grand National ten years before his epic win on Aldaniti, aboard Country Wedding. Tracking the previous year's winner Gay Trip, under Terry Biddlecombe, the partnership was brought down at the first by that horse. The following year, Champion came to grief at the 11th - the open ditch alongside the canal - again on Country Wedding In 1973 he came a creditable sixth of 17 finishers on 100-1 outsider, Hurricane Rock. Having started his career at Toby Balding's yard, before going freelance, he secured a retainer with Josh Gifford in 1974 and came sixth in the National on Manicou Bay. His next four rides yielded a 14th place on Money Market in 1976, a first fence fall with Spittin' Image in '77 and falls from both Shifting Gold and Purdo at the next two runnings. In 1980, the year before he won, he was seriously ill with cancer. Having left the Royal Marsden Hospital in an emaciated state, he put on four stone in weight in three months and helped cover the big race for the BBC.

Amateur Riders

Below:
Tommy Pickernell,
aka Mr. Thomas

In the first three official runnings of the race, from 1839 to 1842, the jockeys were actually supposed to be amateur 'gentleman riders', though only about half actually were. For much of the history of the great race, amateur riders have done remarkably well in this major sporting contest. Thirty nine have won the race, but only five since the end of the Second World War, the last of which was Old Etonian Marcus Armytage on the Kim Bailey-trained Mr. Frisk in 1990. He may well have been the final Corinthian to do so, and also set what will probably be an all-time course record over the modified fences, on an un-watered course. The time was eight minutes 47.8 seconds.

Three amateurs won it three times in the early days: Thomas

Below:
Tommy Pickernell,
aka Mr. Thomas

Pickernell (aka Mr. Thomas) with Anatis in 1860, The Lamb (1871) and

Pathfinder (1875); Tommy Beasley on Empress (1880), Woodbrook (1881) and Frigate (1889); and Jack Anthony with Glenside (1911), Ally Sloper (1915) and Troytown (1920). Three amateurs have won it twice: Alec Goodman on Miss Mowbray (1852) and Salamander (1866); John Maunsell Richardson on Disturbance (1873) and Reugny (1874); and Ted Wilson on Voluptuary (1884) and Roquefort (1885). In the post war period Capt. Bobby Petre won in 1946 on Lovely Cottage; American Tommy Smith on Jay Trump, in 1965; fellow American Charlie Fenwick with Ben Nevis, in 1980; and two years later Dick Saunders with Grittar; with Armytage the last in 1990.

Facts in History

The jockey to have ridden in the most Nationals is Tom Olliver, who rode 19 times between the first running in 1839 to 1859. A.P.McCoy announced he would retire at the end of the season in February 2015. At that stage he was on 18 rides, so would never beat Olliver's record.

The horse to have run most is Manifesto, eight times between 1895 and 1904.

The 1985 winner Last Suspect ran in the Arkle colours of Anne, Duchess of Wesminster. She had never let Arkle contest the National.

After some poor pre-National runs both trainer Tim Forster and the owner were set to withdraw him from the big race. It was jockey, Hywel Davies, who persuaded connections to go ahead.

The Sefton Suite at the Adelphi Hotel, Liverpool, long-time favourite of racegoers, was refurbished in 1912 as a replica of the smoking lounge on the Titanic. Between the wars, hotel alcoves at the postrace celebrations were decorated as Aintree fences and partygoers would slide down the staircase on waiters' silver trays. Roy Rogers' horse Trigger stayed at the Adelphi three weeks before the National in 1954.

Bomb scare

In 1997, at the running of the 150th Grand National, two calls at 2.49 pm and 2.52 pm warned that a bomb would be detonated at the race course at 4.00 pm.

The Irish voice used a recognised IRA codeword. After the 2.55 race the course was on alert and at 3.16 all 60,000 people on the course, including jockeys, bookies and caterers, had to abandon their work stations and leave all their belongings behind.

Six thousand vehicles also had to be left at Aintree overnight to be checked out by police. J.P. McManus had to leave his betting stash in a private box.

The Tote had to leave half a million pounds in cash on the course, though one of their reps managed to cram £7,000 into her panties, so as not to leave it in her booth. Makes you proud! Fifty horses would have been left unattended until 6.00 pm had two stable lads not refused to leave - and fed and watered them all. Local hotels, churches and gyms all played host to refugee race-goers.

The National was rescheduled for 5.00pm on the Monday. Some members of the public vandalised the jumps and rails, so a certain amount of repair work had to be carried out on the Sunday. The postponed race was won by Lord Gyllene.

Far Left:
Lord Gyllene and
Tony Dobbin

Left:
Post race
crowds desperse

Facts in History

The first National was held on a Tuesday and attracted an estimated crowd of 40,000. This dropped by about 10,000 for several years, but picked up again at the end of the century. The biggest estimated crowd was after WW2 when over 300,000 war-weary race-goers are thought to have turned up. For many years the race was run on a Friday but since the switch to Saturday in 1947 the lowest figure was 9,000 in 1975 and now averages about 70,000.

Charles Barnett's first Grand National after he took over as managing director of Aintree in 1993 was the year of the shambolic start and void race. From this inauspicious baptism of fire he proved to be an inspired boss, overseeing the total revamping of facilities just before his departure to Ascot in 2007. Ginger McCain remarked of his departure, 'I have nothing but complete and utter admiration for the man, but he's a dirty rotten, windy bastard for going down south to Ascot.'

Films

There have been two feature films to use the Grand National as the backdrop for the action: *National Velvet* and *Champions*. *National Velvet* started life as a book published by Enid Bagnold in 1935, and told the story of horse-mad teenager Velvet Brown, who dreamed of riding in the Grand National. The film is set in an idyllic England with Velvet, the daughter of a butcher, winning a coloured horse in a raffle. A year later she is lining up for the Grand National. So far so likely! In the book the descriptions of Aintree are fairly realistic, even down to Velvet seeing naked jockeys in the weighing room. It was an inspiring fantasy however, which certainly fired lady riders (and indeed trainers) to have dreams of Aintree glory.

In 1944 Hollywood hired an all-star cast with a young Elizabeth Taylor as Velvet. Having won 'The Pie' in the raffle she is helped in the training by a young, penniless drifter, Mi Taylor, played by Mickey Rooney, who turns up at the Browns having found the name and address among his late father's belongings. The Browns invite him in; Mrs. Brown keeps quiet about the connection, but she persuades her husband to let him stay around to help with the horse and their daughter's ambition to run him in the big race. It turns out that Mi was a northern jockey whose career had ended in a racecourse collision, in which the other jockey had died. Mi went off the rails and now actively hates horses. Cue time for atonement. The film's abbreviation of the horse's name (The Piebald) to "Pie" was meant to be short for Pirate, since he had jumped out of his paddock and caused mayhem in the village, so was put up for the fateful raffle.

Mi and Velvet duly train The

MICKEY ROONEY   ELIZABETH TAYLOR

NATIONAL VELVET

Right:
*John Hurt,
Champion*

Pie for the National, with the intention of putting up a real jockey for the race. The night before, however, Velvet thinks the intended rider doesn't rate his chances and gets Mi to stand him down. This leaves the former washed-out jockey to get his bottle back and take the ride, but Velvet has other ideas and decides to pretend to be a boy and take the ride herself.

Hollywood then takes enormous liberties with the race itself. Shot in California, the jumps look nothing like Aintree's formidable obstacles, the field comprises a veritable United Nations of competitors and they go faster than a five-furlong sprint on the flat, though the film extends the race to five miles.

Avoiding mid-race rough and tumble, Pie and Velvet come in first past the post. Velvet however is so excited she faints and falls off. The doctor rumbles that she is a girl and they are disqualified, but The Pie has proved himself and the Brown family become a media sensation, with offers of Hollywood stardom.

Mi leaves but not before having been told that his father had long ago been Mrs. Brown's trainer when she had been the first woman to swim the channel.

Liz Taylor did actually ride 'Pie' (in reality a gelding, King Charles) in many scenes, but her stunt double was an Australian jockey, Snowy Baker. Taylor was given the horse by MGM for her thirteenth birthday.

Champions (1983) is a biopic telling the true story of Bob Champion's remarkable fightback from testicular cancer to ride the equally injury-compromised Aldaniti to victory in the 1981 Grand National. Only two years after the real thing, it was slightly odd seeing actors playing people who were very recognisable but unlike *National Velvet* every effort was made to make the action shots look realistic. Actual footage of the real race was used and high-definition action from 1983 also spliced in. Several professional jockeys earned some pocket money as stunt riders, including the late John Burke, National-winning rider in 1976, who rode as Champion.

Trainer Josh Gifford was portrayed by Edward Woodward, with British character actor Peter Barkworth playing owner Nick Embiricos. The lead was played by John Hurt, famous for *The Elephant Man* and his portrayal of Quentin Crisp in *The Naked Civil Servant*,. He was excellent and won an award at the 1985 Evening Standard British Film Awards for his role. Even though relatively young, Hurt had a somewhat lived-in face and voice, and playing the ailing Champion probably looked worse than the man himself. Certainly when Bob

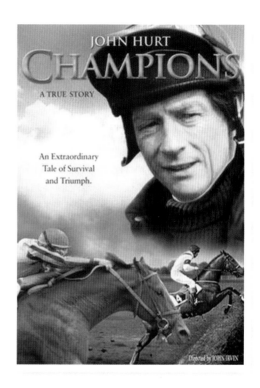

had got himself fit to ride in the race in 1981 he looked in much better nick than Hurt in the film.

In a nice touch, Aldaniti played himself in the movie.

Sponsors

In the early days of racing the prize pot was made up from the entry fees. Commercial sponsorship in horseracing only started in 1957 when former Grand National Corinthian Colonel Bill Whitbread put up money for the Whitbread Gold Cup. In 1958 the National was taken on by the Irish Hospital Sweepstakes, with £5,000 contributed to the prize fund. In 1961 and '62 Schweppes added a similar amount, but then shifted their contribution to their own Gold Trophy at the same meeting. Vaux Breweries, who also put in £5,000, took over with the Irish Sweepstakes in 1963, but by 1965 the Grand National was starting its 'last ever' phase.

In 1972 BP put up £10,000 and in 1974 the property company who had now bought the racecourse from the Topham family, the Walton Group, doubled this. The 1973 first win of Red Rum and subsequent triumphs gave the race a lifeline of publicity.

Ladbrokes took on the administration of the race for seven years in 1975.

£40,000 then came from the *News of the World* newspaper from 1975 to 1977 and transferred to the group's daily stable mate the *Sun* in 1978.

Sponsorship was still almost on a year by year basis, which would have put enormous pressure on the executive. Yet another one off sponsor took over for 1979 (Colt Car) and then the *Sun* came in again until 1983.

The Ladbrokes deal had come to an end, and again the race was in crisis. A public appeal to save the race had failed, but a saviour came in the form of Canadian distillers Seagram, who injected serious money under their UK Chairman Ivan Straker.

This now put the course in the

Above:
John Smith's
big beer can

hands of what is now known as Jockey Club Racecourses. Seagram put up the prize money of up to £55,000 and continued to support the race until 1991.

The race sponsorship was then taken over by Martell Cognac (a subsidiary of Seagram's) and the big race was known as The Martell Grand National until 2004. At the end of their tenure Seagram had contributed about £25,000,000 to the Grand National cause.

In 2005 another brewer, Scottish and Newcastle, took over and branded the race The John Smith's Grand National, and they remained as sponsors until 2013.

From 2014 the race has been sponsored by Crabbie's, another drinks company, most famous for their adult 'alcoholic Ginger Beer'.

Indeed, the owners Halewood International have a special affiliation with Aintree and the Grand National, as they are based in the heart of Liverpool.

The company's Chairwoman, Judy Halewood, has been passionately involved in the race since 1991 when she was the first ever female to own, train and breed a horse for the National - Harley - who finished a respectable 12th that year.

Halewood also own Amberleigh House who won the race in 2004 to seal legendary trainer Ginger McCain's fourth Grand National title. During Amberleigh House's career, the top-class chaser competed 11 times over the Grand National fences.

This association was extended in 2014, with the last-minute addition of Halewood International-owned horse Swing Bill, trained by David Pipe, who finished in ninth place, allowing the Halewood family to once more enjoy the excitement of the race, as both sponsor and owner.

In 2014, the inaugural year as title sponsor, Crabbie's really put their mark on the world's greatest steeplechase with a record £1million purse for the first time in its celebrated history.

A new trophy was designed to usher in a new era for the world's greatest steeplechase with a minimalistic design in the form of a horse's head, reflecting the modern approach that Crabbie's is bringing to the Grand National Festival.

Peter Eaton Snr., Deputy Chairman at Halewood International, announced a new charity partnership with Help for Heroes in 2015: "As the 40 horses and jockeys line up to race across the famous fences, this year will again prove to be another thrilling adventure for all involved and one of the country's greatest sporting moments. There are exciting times ahead for the company, Aintree and Help for Heroes."

Facts in History

Top Right:
*The Old
Weighing Room*

Top Far Right:
*The new
Weighing Room*

Below:
*Grandstand view of
the course*

The National has been run on Monday (1997), Tuesday, Wednesday and Thursday but from 1876 until 1946 was run on a Friday. In 1947 it switched to a Saturday running (the last day of the three-day meeting), with the exception of 1957 when it reverted to a Friday in a fruitless attempt to boost falling attendances.

Aintree racecourse covers about 250 acres.

2006 saw the new paddock and weighing room and 2007 the new stands. The Old Weighing Room is now the Winners' Bar and part of the Aintree Museum.

The Duke of Alberquerque, also known as Beltran de Osorio y Diez de Rivera had his last of several National rides and crashes at the age of 57, when tighter medical strictures ruled him out. He had broken 22 bones in his racing career and reckoned to have sustained 107 fractures just at Aintree. He first rode in the National in 1952 and came back 11 years later. He did complete the race.

The second fence was at one time called Fan's Fence after a mare of that name who refused there three years running. Fan had actually jumped the obstacle to finish second in 1867 but persistently declined to go further in 1868, '69 and '70.

Despite a frighteningly high attrition rate with jockey deaths in the early years of steeplechasing, James Wynne, in 1862, was the only one to lose his life in the National. Sadly, several successful Aintree riders perished on other courses soon after their National triumph. These tended to be over smaller but faster courses. The 1854 winning jockey John Tasker, on Bourton, was killed at Warwick. William Watkinson died in a £100 chase at Bogside in Scotland three weeks after winning the National with Jack Horner, and Billy Speck, third in 1935 on Thomond II, died in the first race at Cheltenham the following year.

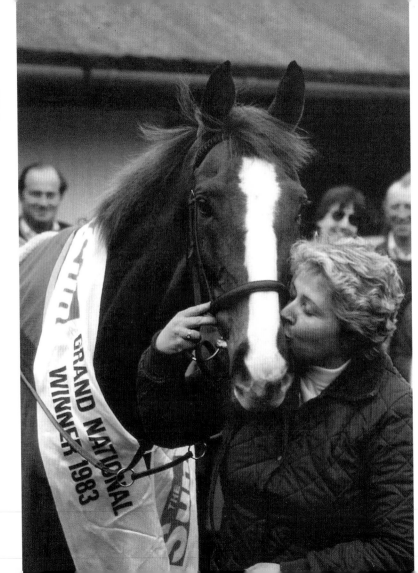

Right:
Corbiere and
Jenny Pitman

Jenny Pitman

Born in 1946, Jennifer Harvey was one of many girls inspired by the film *National Velvet*, where Elizabeth Taylor trained and surreptitiously rode her horse 'The Pie' to victory in the National.

Jenny was one of seven children who grew up on a farm in Leicestershire with no power or running water. She first sat on a pony when she was only fourteen months old. Her stockman father David trained a few point-to-pointers and gave Jenny her first ride when she was fifteen, on a horse called Dan Archer. Her father, by profession good with animals, had a good eye for a horse and in later years accompanied Jenny to sales well into her training career.

She married jockey Richard Pitman in 1965 when still in her teens, and they set up a successful point-to-point livery yard. Richard's career was on the up. He came second in the National in 1969 on Steel Bridge and more famously four years later on the gallant Crisp who led all the way in 1973, only to be caught at the last gasp by Red Rum. He was also winning other big races. The marriage broke down however and Jenny found herself trying to run a yard and bring up the two sons of the marriage. She seriously considered chucking it all in to work in a shoe shop, but was persuaded to stick to it by Fred Winter. She moved to Weathercock House in Upper Lambourn and turned the ramshackle set-up into a top yard.

Her first success from here under Rules was in 1975 and she won her first big race, the Midlands National, in 1977. It was that year, when Red Rum was taking all the headlines for his third win in the greatest steeplechase, that Mrs. Pitman had her first runner in the Grand National. The Songwriter, a 200-1 outsider, was owned by a real songwriter, P.R.Callander, whose biggest hit was The Ballad of Bonnie and Clyde. He also wrote for Tony Christie and Cliff Richard. His horsewas pulled up before the second Becher's. (Jenny kept the music links, later training horses for Errol Brown from the band Hot Chocolate).

In 1978 The Songwriter

completed to finish twelfth and the next year Jenny had a good chance with Artistic Prince until he fell at the 26th. The following season she really began to make her mark, with Bueche winning six races, and was forging a reputation as a top trainer of long distance chasers.

A portent of things to come materialised in 1982 when Corbiere won the Welsh National at Chepstow. The following year Jenny made history by becoming the first winning lady trainer of the Grand National when Corbiere came in under Ben de Haan. The following spring she consolidated her reputation by training Burrough Hill Lad to lift the Cheltenham Gold Cup. That year and the next Corbiere finished third in the National.

Burrough Hill Lad was entered in 1988 but didn't run, and her other entry, Smith's Man, pulled up at the third. She then had ninth-placed Team Challenge and

Gainsay, ridden by son Mark in his first National ride. They fell at the 19th. Mark however did win the Cheltenham Gold Cup for her in 1991 on Garrison Savannah. He looked good to win the National too that year, landing in front over the last, only to be beaten by the appropriately named Seagram.

In 1993 Mrs. Pitman had three runners – two fancied entries, Garrison Savannah and Royal Athlete, and Esha Ness. After a botched start the race became a farce when some of the field kept going for the whole two circuits and the race was declared void.

The 'winner' was Esha Ness under John White. Frustratingly, Esha Ness's time was the second fastest completion ever.

In 1995 Jenny fielded no fewer than six of the 35 starters, among them Royal Athlete, with whom she really wanted to bypass Aintree and go for the Scottish National. Owner

Left:
Corbiere and
Ben de Haan

pressure persuaded her to run him at Aintree, and he triumphed at 40-1. She also trained the winner of the Scottish National that year, Willsford.

In 1996 the Richard Dunwoody ridden Superior Finish did indeed live up to his name by storming to third place and the following year Mudahim won the Irish National for her, giving her a clean sweep of Welsh, Scottish, Irish and Aintree Nationals. It was a big year for Jenny, being awarded the OBE and marrying her long time partner David Stait. In Dick Francis style she has also put her name to several racing thrillers.

Pranks and Scrapes

Right:
Steve Smith-Eccles

Jockey Steve Smith Eccles, one of the weighing room's comedians, had an interesting start to the 1986 Aintree meeting. He was cross at being beaten in an early race on River Ceirog, who had won the Supreme Novices Hurdle at Cheltenham by 40 lengths, so he hit the Scotch, and continued to do when he repaired to his room at The Royal Clifton, Southport, which he was sharing with his girlfriend Di Haine. They had a row, so he went off drinking with pals and decided on his return not to risk Di's wrath again, opting instead to sleep it off in the back of his Mercedes parked in the street outside. He woke up to find himself speeding down a dual carriageway courtesy of a joy rider who had nicked his car. Steve had a dilemma. If he went 'boo!' the driver might panic and write them both off. He went for it, and the joy rider screeched to a halt, leapt out and ran away. Steve drove back to the hotel and went back to sleep with the car keys in his pocket. Understandably happy to regale this yarn the following day, the media had a great story. An amusing yarn for a Corinthian amateur but perhaps not the most professional approach for a paid rider! Smith Eccles however acquitted himself well in the big race coming third on Classified. On another occasion, out of contention on Zongalero, he was alongside Tommy McGivern on Drumroan who was telling a joke. Sadly Drumroan fell before the punch line. As McGivern was scooping himself off the deck, Eccles reappeared. Zongalero had stopped at the next, so the jockey rode back to find out how the joke had ended.

Dave Dick, winner on ESB in the 'Devon Loch' year, 1956, was lined up at the start one year and spotted a banner stating: 'Repent or your sins will find you out'. Dick remarked to a fellow jockey, 'If that's the case I won't get as far as the first.'

Trainer Nicky Henderson once received a fax on Aintree-headed paper saying that all mares were to be banned from the race a couple of days hence, as they would distract the geldings. He was running a mare, Fiddling the Facts. Momentarily shocked at this very late change in the rules, he noticed the date: April 1. In another April Fool's spoof, The Sporting Life ran a piece saying that trainer Kim Bailey's event-riding wife Tracey was to ride the previous year's winner, Mr. Frisk, in lieu of the successful Marcus Armytage. Outraged trainer John Webber said he would offer Marcus the ride on

his Auntie Dot. In the end Marcus pulled up Mr. Frisk and Auntie Dot came third under Mark Dwyer. As it happens, Tracey did compete on Mr. Frisk but long after he had retired from racing.

Nigel Payne

Nigel was instrumental in re-establishing the profile of the National over a twenty year period. He had his problem days, including the void race of 1993 and the bomb scare and postponement in 1997. Ever the consummate PR man, he came into his own in the void year when a big media backlash became inevitable.

Aintree Chairman Lord Daresbury, managing director of the racecourse Charles Barnett, David Hillyard (representing course owners, Racecourse Holdings Trust) and Payne needed a crisis meeting. They were being pestered for discussions by the Jockey Club's head of security, Roger Buffham, who they didn't want to be party to their debrief. Nigel steered Buffham to the Grosvenor Hotel, Chester, but the quartet actually met in Daresbury's dining room.

Nigel owns an empty pack of Josh Gifford's B&H cigarettes. The trainer pledged to give up the weed if Aldaniti

won. When he did, Gifford gave his half-full pack to Payne, who smoked the fags but kept the packet as a souvenir.

Nigel's early shoe-in as Grand National press-man engendered a genuine love for the race. In 1992 he got a syndicate of six together to buy a four-year-old gelding for 5,800 guineas. His great chum, football commentator John Motson, declined the offer to become a partner in the ownership.

A year after buying the horse, Nigel backed him at 33-1 for £100 each way to win the National by the year 2000. The horse was Earth Summit and he duly obliged in 1998. The horse also set a record for winning both the Welsh and Scottish Nationals in addition to the "real thing".

Void National

1993 will go down in National history for ignominious reasons. The starting procedure for a race with so many runners was always a challenge for the organisers. In the early days it was just started with the drop of a flag; for a race of its four-and-a-half mile length, probably the best low-tech way of seeing them off.

For many years however a head high starting tape had been employed across the 80-yard width of the course, which sprung up and away when the Starter pulled a lever. It was a somewhat antiquated system, with modern jockeys bunching up and being told on many occasions to 'take a turn'.

In 1993 the comedy of errors began when, for some reason, the 39 runners were let out on to the course 25 minutes before the 'Off'. The start of the Grand National is always a tense affair, and too much milling about at the start was bound to up the ante. On paper there were

Below:
Up goes the
flag in 1993

Above:
A distressed
John White
(yellow and green)

now ten minutes after the parade in which to line up, and both horse and rider nerves were jangling. All they wanted to do was to get going.

There was then a further delay when animal rights protesters had to be removed from the first fence. There was also a false claim that a firebomb had been planted at Becher's. A perfect storm was brewing. The horses were down at

the start too early and then lined up a full nine minutes late.

When Starter Capt. Keith Brown pulled the lever, the light tape blew back into the cavalry charge and got entangled with several runners. Brown called a false start. What Jenny Pitman described as 'the knicker elastic' had failed to do its job.

Down by the first fence the false

start flag-man, Ken Evans, waved his red ensign. All runners managed to pull up. Back they went to line up again. At 4.03pm Capt. Brown pulled his lever again. This was worse. The tape got caught under the head of Judy Davies' ride, Formula One, and round the neck of former-winning jockey Richard Dunwoody.

The cry of 'false start' went up again and Brown stuck up his flag. It failed to unfurl, so Evans at the first let 30 of the 39 who had decided to set off continue past him on a four-and-a-half mile road to nowhere.

Officials and connections tried in vain to wave them down, and after one circuit 12 did pull up. There were seven still ploughing on, however. Esha Ness, the least fancied of Jenny Pitman's runners, came home in front under John White for a result which was never going to stand. To make the disappointment worse, the horse had achieved the second-ever fastest time round the course.

Captain Brown needed a police escort to leave the racecourse, but in many respects it was the outdated technology that caused the mayhem. Brown had even advised the racecourse the previous year that the system needed improvement.

The start is now conducted in a much more fluid and less frantic way and is probably no better or worse than the old fashioned flag start.

Below:
Starter Keith Brown needs protection

Venetia Williams

Venetia was one of the pioneering lady jockeys to ride in the Grand National, though her attempt ended on the grass on the landing side of Becher's when she parted company from Marcolo in 1988. The horse did a somersault and Venetia was knocked out. Two weeks later she broke her neck in a fall and was lucky to survive. She spent three months in hospital. That was the end of riding in races. She went to work for Martin Pipe and Barry Hills, Colin Hayes, and as assistant to John Edwards.

Venetia set up her own yard in 1995 and won the Hennessy Gold Cup in 1998 with Teeton Mill.

She had two runners in the 1997 National, Don't Light Up who came down at the 13th, and Celtic Abbey, who dropped Richard Johnson at The Chair. The latter fell the following year under Norman Williamson. She had her first completion in 1999 with General Wolfe, who was brought down in 2001 while her other runner that year, Inis Cara fell at the fourthand pulled up at the second Canal Turn in 2002.

Venetia was doing well as a trainer, but Aintree was not proving a lucky course for her. She had several other disappointments, but this all changed in 2009 when Mon Mome came storming in for her, making her only the second lady trainer to win the National after Jenny Pitman.

Venetia is unique in being the only lady to have both ridden in, and trained a Grand National winner.

Fashion

Right:
Nice buns

Below:
Aintree's finest

At many race meetings now, the Royal Ascot idea of a Ladies' Day has taken hold. Aintree's is usually on the Friday before the

National, but local style pervades the meeting. On cold April days Liverpool's finest parade their tans, heels, inks and embonpoints.

On being asked by a TV reporter whether she was not feeling cold, a sporting race-goer responded, 'Of course not. I'm wearing two thongs.'

End Piece

From its early runnings, when the Grand National complemented the then-more popular Waterloo Cup as a great northern sporting occasion, it has evolved into one of the world's greatest spectacles. This Little Book of the Grand National has chronicled some of the extraordinary feats of riding, training, equine heroics, fairytales, disasters, characters and frankly unbelievable tales of derring-do and romance. The race was run for the 'last' time several times, massive fields sometimes produced just a handful of finishers, but Aintree has always risen to the challenge to modernise and develop. It is a fine line between making the event too 'safe' and providing a challenge, which keeps a more sensitive sporting audience enjoying the bravery of horse and rider in the 21st century. What is unique about the Grand National is that it can still produce historic tales. There will be many more to come.

Below:
All action

About the Author

Julian Seaman has written for many
equestrian magazines.

He is Media Director of the Mitsubishi Motors
Badminton Horse Trials and was Venue
Media Manager during the Olympic Games at
Greenwich. A former international Three Day
Event rider, Julian also rode the Grand National
fences in the Foxhunters Chase in 1988.

This his eighth equestrian book, which
include Little Book of Badminton and
Little Book of Eventing.

**The pictures in this book were provided
courtesy of the Press Association**

www.pressassociation.com

Book design by Flokk Creative
www.flokkcreative.co.uk

Written and researched by Julian Seaman,
with special thanks to Jane Clarke

Published by G2 Entertainment
Publishers Edward Adams & Jules Gammond

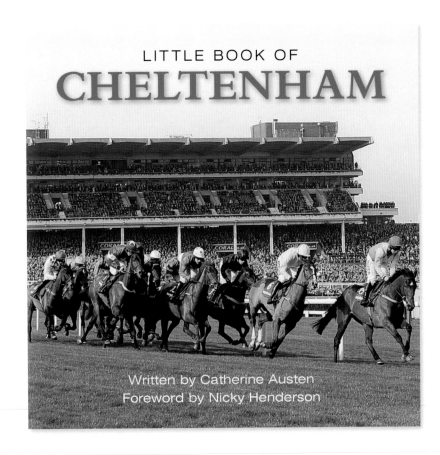

LITTLE BOOK OF
CHELTENHAM

Written by Catherine Austen
Foreword by Nicky Henderson